B"H

BAAL SHEM TOV

RABBI YISRAEL BEN ELIEZER
THE LEGENDARY KABBALAH MASTER

HOLY DAYS

MYSTICAL STORIES ON
SABBATH AND YOM TOV

VOLUME VI

Compiled and Freely Adapted
By **Tzvi Meir Cohn**

BST Publishing
Cleveland, Ohio

ISBN: 978-0-9792865-3-7

Library of Congress Control Number: 2011962166
Library of Congress subject heading:
1. Chassidim — Legends. 2. Baal Shem Tov, ca. 1700-1760 — Legends. 3. Chassidism. 4. Mysticism Judaism. 5. Title.

BST Publishing
Cleveland, OH 44124
info@bstpublishing.com
www.bstpublishing.com

Rabbi Sholom Ber Chaikin

Chabad - Lubavitch Community - Cleveland

2480 Beachwood Blvd.
Beachwood, Ohio 44122

Tel. (216) 381-9178 • Fax (216) 381-0443

שלום דובער חייקין

רב

דק' חב"ד – ליובאוויטש

קליוולאנד, אהייא

B"H   14 Adar II 5771

"It is a Mitzvah to publicize those people who perform Mitzvos."

Reb Tzvi Meir HaCohane Cohn, who lives here in Cleveland, has invested tremendous efforts, both monetarily and with his time, to publicize the Torah and stories of the Holy Baal Shem Tov. With regards to his present project of publicizing stories that relate to the weekly Torah portion, I express many thanks and gratitude for his undertaking this wonderful endeavor, L'sheim Shamayim (for the sake of Heaven). To emphasize his holy work, I would like to share with you from the words of the Previous Chabad Rebbe, which are printed in the sefer Igros Kodesh Admur Harayatz ZATZAL , Vol. 6. as follows:

S. B. Chaikin

Rabbi Sholom Ber Chaikin

IGROS KODESH Vol. 6
written by the Previous Rebbe[1]

As the well known story goes, the Tzemach Tzedek[2] once sent his truly brilliant Chassid, the famed Rav Yitzchak Aizik HaLevi Epstein from Homil, to the Rebbe of Ruzhin,[3] regarding matters that pertained to the community. This Chassid, who was one of the educated ones of the Chabad Chassidim, was very interested to learn the ways and customs of the Rhyzhiner Chassidim and especially the customs of the Rebbe, Reb Yisrael of Ruzhin, and therefore he put his incredible mind and heart to observe every little detail of what happened.

The way the Holy Rhyzhiner Rebbe would accept people and read the kvitlach,[4] which was the

---

[1]Rabbi Yosef Yitzchak Schneerson [1880-1950], the sixth Rebbe of Chabad-Lubavitch.
[2]Rabbi Menachem Mendel Schneerson [1789-1886], the third Rebbe of Chabad-Lubavitch.
[3]Rabbi Yisrael Friedmann of Ruzhin [1797-1850] was a great-grandson of the Maggid of Mezritch. At a young age was already a charismatic leader with a large following of Chassidim. Greatly respected by the other Rebbes and Jewish leaders of his generation, he was - and still is - referred to as "The Holy Rhyzhiner."
[4]Written petitions for blessings and prayers placed on pieces of paper.

general way by Chassidim of Poland and Vohlin, was as follows. There would be one chosen Chassid selected from the Chassidic elders by the Rebbe, who would be the translator between the Rebbe and his Chassidim. He was called the "close one". This person would stand on the Rebbe's right side to greet people and receive the kvitlach while the gabbai[5] rishon would stand to the left of the Rebbe.

One of the guests at that time in Ruzhin was one of the great Rabbis in Bukavinya, known as a great scholar, and among the closest followers of the Holy Rhyzhiner Rebbe. He brought his sefer, a book of Torah insights to get a haskomah (approbation) from the Rebbe.

Also among the guests was a Chassid who had gathered stories of Tzaddikim and Chassidim over the years and he also brought a sefer containing a compilation of these stories to get a haskomah from the Rebbe.

The time came when the Rebbe was receiving people and these two, the Rav and the Chassid, were standing before the Rebbe with their books. The designated Chassid intermediary, as instructed

---

[5]A person who assists in the running of a synagogue and ensures that the needs are met or an administrator to a rabbi (particularly the secretary or personal assistant to a Chassidic Rebbe).

by the Rebbe, took both books and read for the Rebbe several random pages from the book of the Rav and then a few stories from the book of the Chassid.

The Rebbe sat there in a state of devekus[6] and then started to speak about the greatness of stories of Tzaddikim and the great impression that these stories make in the heichalos (chambers) of the Tzaddikim in Gan Eden. And afterwards, he expounded on the Torah insights that had been read to him from the book of the Rav. He then instructed the interpreter to write his haskomah for both of these books.

The Chabad Chassid, Rav Yitzchak Aizik, was carefully observing the unfolding of these events, the manner in which the Rebbe was receiving the people and how he would relate to his followers. He was amazed at the depth of analysis that the Rebbe offered on the insights that were read to him from the book of the Rav.

He was, however, confused by the fact that the Rebbe had addressed his comments and given his haskomah for the story book before commenting on and giving his haskomah for the book of the Rav. He found this to be quite surprising.

---

[6]Meditative state of being close to G•d.

Two days later was Rosh Chodesh and the Tzemach Tzedek's Chassid, Reb Aizik, was invited to the seudah of Reb Yisrael, the Holy Ryzhiner Rebbe. During the seudah, the Rebbe spoke words of Torah and before the benching[7], he said as follows:

"The Litvish Gaon (referring to Reb Aizik) found it surprising that we first spoke about the stories of the Tzaddikim and only afterwards about the sefer containing chiddushei Torah (insights in Torah), and also, that we gave our approval for an haskomah to the book of stories before the book of chiddushei Torah.

"This, in truth, is a great and old question that was asked by Rashi HaKadosh[8], who was a Goan Olam (world class Torah scholar) in the revealed and hidden aspects of Torah. He asked this same question on the first verse in Bereishis. His question was that the Torah only needed to start from the verse of "This month is for you."[9] What is the reason that the Torah starts with Bereishis? He answered, it is to tell of the strength of His (G•d's) deeds. This refers to the neshamah (soul) which is

---

[7] Prayers after eating a meal.
[8] Rabbi Shlomo Itzhaki (1040-1105).
[9] The first mitzvah given to the Jewish people.

in every action within creation at every time and at every moment."

"The Zaide, the holy great Maggid,[10] received from the holy Baal Shem Tov a way to see in everything the neshamah (soul) that is in the body of that thing."

"You understand," he turned to the Chassid, Rav Yitzchak Aizik, "we emulate the order that Hashem gave us in his holy Torah. First, Sefer Bereishis is the stories of Tzaddikim. As the Medrash says, "With whom did Hashem consult, with the Neshamos of the Tzaddikim." Only afterwards do we have sefer Shemos in which it is stated "HaChodesh hazeh lachem."[11]

"Both of the authors are Chassidim of stature. Both manuscripts are wondrous chiddushim. The chiddushim of Torah authored by the Rav attest to the great learning and thought that the author brought to light in the Holy Torah. And the stories of the Tzaddikim attest to the great novelty that Hashem brought to light in the world. Therefore, we preceded the haskomah for the sefer of stories of Tzaddikim to that of the haskomah for the sefer of Torah insights."

---

[10] Rabbi Dov Ber of Mezeritch (1704-1772).
[11] "This month is to you . . . " (Exodus 12:2).

G•D

Dedicated to the millions of Chassidim and their Rebbes, who for nearly three centuries, have cherished and passed these holy stories down to us.

יברכך יי וישמרך

יאר יי פניו אליך ויחנך

ישא יי פניו אליך וישם לך שלום

"May the L•rd bless you and guard you. May the L•rd make His countenance shine upon you and be gracious to you. May the L•rd turn His countenance towards you and grant you peace."

SHALOM AND BLESSINGS

Faith Love Joy
Faith Love Joy
Faith Love Joy Faith
Faith Love Joy
Joy Faith Love Joy
Faith Love Joy
Faith Love Joy
G•d
Faith Love Joy
Faith Love Joy

**Yisrael Ben Moreinu Rabbeinu HaRav Rav
Eliezer KoesB (presently in) Mezibush**
Signature of the Baal Shem Tov

BST
Publishing

TABLE OF CONTENTS

INTRODUCTION

The most famous master of Kabbalah[12] and Jewish mysticism is Rabbi Yisrael Ben Eliezer. Rabbi Yisrael lived from 1698 to 1760, and is known as the Baal Shem Tov.[13] More stories are told about the Baal Shem Tov than about any other person in Jewish history. These stories have been passed down, primarily through an oral tradition, for over 250 years. More recently, books — and even more recently the internet — have been added as a means to continue the time—honored tradition of transmitting Baal Shem Tov stories from parent to child and from Chassid[14] to Chassid.

The Baal Shem Tov stories are indeed glimpses of the life and culture of downtrodden, 18th century, Eastern European Jewry. However, to see

---

[12] Jewish Mystical Tradition.
[13] Master of the Good Name.
[14] A Chassid is a pious person — one who goes "beyond the line of the law" in his duties toward G•d and man.

the stories as only that is to miss their central role. In Chassidic life, Baal Shem Tov stories have formed the foundation of one of the most fundamental and important of Chassidic spiritual practices: telling stories about the Tzaddikim — the Jewish saints, as it were; literally, the "righteous ones"—the great Spiritual Masters. These Tzaddikim led and guided the various Chassidic dynasties through the dark exile of European Jewry, from the time of the Baal Shem Tov.

All Chassidim, irrespective of their particular allegiance — whether to Chabad, Bretslov, Aleksander, Belz, Satmar, Gerrer, Vishnitz, to name a few — share one common belief: that the basic facts of the Baal Shem Tov stories are just that — facts. There is an old Chassidic saying: "If you believe all of the Baal Shem Tov stories you're a fool; if you don't believe any of them you are a bigger fool."

Today, the stories and teachings of the Baal Shem Tov are as relevant as they were in the past. They inspire and guide us. They nudge us towards intensifying our service to G•d.[15] The stories teach through example how to live our life with a joyful

---

[15] It is a practice among practicing Jews not to spell out the Name of the Almighty.

attitude. They enable us to experience the flow of love that emanates from G•d.

I would like to express my gratitude to many people who have made this book possible.

Rabbi Sholom Ber Chaikin for reading the manuscript of this book, checking for errors and catching various mistakes of fact and occasionally tone.

To my ever supportive wife, my best friend and muse Basha, thank you.

May G•d, blessed be He, shower blessings on all those who have helped in the preparation of this book.

PREFACE

BAAL SHEM TOV literally means, "Master of the Good Name." How appropriate an appellation for Rabbi Yisrael ben Eliezer, who was to become the founder of the Chassidic movement — the single most important religious movement in Jewish history! We know that he was born on the 18th of Elul in 1698 and left this world on Shavuos, the 6th of Sivan in 1760, but little other verifiable biographical information has come down to us. Moreover, the Baal Shem Tov's life is so overlain with legend, it is difficult to determine what is true of the information we do have.

According to the stories, Rabbi Yisrael's parents were poor, righteous, and hospitable. When he was orphaned at a very young age, the Jewish community of Horodenka took him under its wing, fed and clothed him, and enrolled him in the local cheder.[16]

He is described as an unusually sensitive child, and quite early demonstrated a profound attachment to G•d and to nature. He often wandered in the forests and fields surrounding the village, and spent many hours there, alone, close to the natural world, talking to G•d.

At the age of twelve, he began working as the local cheder teacher's assistant. His job was to bring the students to and from school and to review their lessons with them. Later, he worked as a shamash,[17] a shochet,[18] and a laborer.

Unbeknownst to others, he was also devoted to Torah study and became extremely learned as a Talmid chacham and Kabbalist.

The man who was to become the Baal Shem Tov so successfully concealed his spiritual and scholarly achievements that the great Talmudist, Rabbi Avraham Gershon of Kitov, vehemently opposed R. Yisrael's marriage to his sister, Chana. Rabbi Avraham Gershon viewed Rabbi Yisrael, who maintained a pretense of humble ignorance, as

---

[16] A Hebrew day school for young boys.
[17] A caretaker of the synagogue.
[18] A ritual slaughterer.

unworthy of the family. They did however marry, and after they had wed, Rabbi Yisrael worked as a clay digger, a wagon driver, an inn keeper, and a healer.

In fact, the Baal Shem Tov (also know by the acronym the BESHT) was part of a group of hidden holy men and mystics who worked among the "Jewish masses." Certainly, in that place and time, the majority of Jews were ignorant of Torah. By moving among the common Jewish folk without revealing their status as learned men, these hidden "Saints" were able to relate easily to those they would later lead.

From his twenty-sixth to his thirty-sixth birthday, the Baal Shem Tov studied the deepest secrets of the Torah with Achiyah the Shilonite. Achiyah HaShiloni is described as a Heavenly teacher — one who was a Biblical Prophet and the teacher of both King David and Elijah the Prophet.

During Rabbi Yisrael's years of travel as a hidden Saint, he had learned a great deal about folk remedies. Eventually, he combined his practical knowledge of herbs and healing with his mastery of Kabbalah, and his first public appearance was as a Baal Shem — the name given to a few, select, Jewish miracle rabbis that used mystical powers engendered by the Kabbalah, to heal the ill, ward off demons, and predict future events. The Baal Shem Tov was distinguished from the other Baal Shems and the first to be called the Baal Shem Tov because of his remarkable spiritual powers including the ability to see events from afar, predict the future, and look into someone's previous incarnations to help those seeking relief from ailments of the body and soul and therefore became known as the Baal Shem Tov.

The Baal Shem Tov took to visiting the nearby towns and hamlets of Podolia, Volhynia, and Galicia, and began preaching the tenets of Chassidism. The most fundamental teaching of Chassidism, as taught by the Baal Shem Tov, is the omnipresence of G•d. The whole universe is a manifestation of the Divine. This manifestation is not an "Emanation" but a "Portion" of G•d; nothing is separate from G•d. Divine (G•d's) providence is a mantle over all. Therefore, everything in creation, including man, animals, plants and even inanimate objects are directly supervised by G•d.

It follows, then, that all things possess an inner spark of holiness — even something or someone we perceive as evil. Every person, no matter how far he or she has strayed from the ways of G•d, is capable of return; no sinner is damned. The Baal Shem Tov's teachings emphasized constant communion with G•d, and the enthusiasm and joy that are essential to an experiential relationship with Him. These ideas were not altogether new to Judaism, but the manner in which they were presented was little short of revolutionary. The Baal Shem Tov spoke directly to the masses of unlearned[19] Jews. Their task, he told them, was not to be something they were not — for example, learned Talmudists. Rather, their task was to infuse their daily lives with spiritual meaning.

The Baal Shem Tov taught that since G•d's providence extends to all of creation, everything is created and continues to exist because of His intention. As G•d is everywhere and in all things, all actions must be performed with an awareness of His presence, as well as with the love and joy that are integral to such awareness. One's goal in life should be to construct for the Holy One, Blessed be He, a habitation in this physical world. Through this, we will merit to bring the Moshiach, so that the world will be in accordance with G•d's plan.

The following was said by the Rebbe Maharash (fourth Rebbe of Chabad-Lubavitch 1832-1882): "The world makes three errors by thinking that telling stories of the Baal Shem Tov

---

[19] Unschooled in Judaism.

on Motzoei Shabbos[20] ensures one's livelihood. First of all, these stories are not to be limited to the Baal Shem Tov, but should include tales of all our Tzaddikim. Secondly, they should not be told only after Shabbos but at any time. And lastly, telling these stories not only ensures livelihood, but serves as a segulah[21] to ensure we receive an abundance of blessings relating to our children, good health and success in our livelihood."

This teaching of the Rebbe Maharash is believed and acted on by all the various groups of Chassidim and is part of the reason I collected and freely adapted and published the stories in this book. By reading and telling these stories to others, you are promised by a long chain of Chassidic Rebbes that you will receive abundant blessings relating to your children, good health and success in your livelihood.

Please tell these stories to others and give this book to others in order to fulfill the requirement of the Moshiach for the Baal Shem Tov's teachings to become publicly known and revealed throughout the world, and his wellsprings (Torah

---

[20] After Shabbos ends.
[21] Charm or remedy of mystical potency.
.

10

from the Source) dispersed throughout the world so that the Moshiach will quickly reveal himself in our days.

CHAPTER ONE

SHABBOS

THE SHABBOS GUEST

RABBI Eliezer and his wife, Rebbetzyn Sarah, outdid themselves in their observance of the mitzvah of hospitality to guests. It was their custom to invite many guests to their home for Shabbos and Yom Tov, especially those in need. They even employed local villagers to wait on the roads that passed by their little village of Okup, to invite passing travelers to their home.

On the Yom Tov and every Shabbos, Rabbi Eliezer told stories of the holy Jewish Masters to the many guests at their table, discussed the teachings found in the holy Torah, and led the singing of the special songs for the day.

The love and joy with which Rabbi Eliezer and Rebbetzyn Sarah carried out the mitzvah of hospitality to guests did not go unnoticed in the heavenly realms. It was decided by the Heavenly Court to answer Rabbi Eliezer's daily prayer. Every day he prayed, "Master of the Universe, please send someone to lead and inspire the Congregation of Israel."[22] In answer to Rabbi Eliezer's prayers, a

---

[22] The Jewish communities in Eastern Europe were living in dangerous times and under difficult conditions.

very lofty soul was selected to be sent into the world, to serve as a light and guide to the Jewish people. This holy soul was to be raised by Rabbi Eliezer and his wife Rebbetzyn Sarah, who had no children, and were advanced in years.

However, the Angel known to all as the Satan,[23] stepped forward before the Heavenly Court and argued that while Rebbetzyn Sarah was certainly a Tzaddekes,[24] Rabbi Eliezer was not worthy of fathering such a holy soul. He was still untested.

"After all," contended the Satan, "Rabbi Eliezer has not proven that he can withstand the most difficult test of all — loving a fellow Jew who scorns the path of his forefathers, that of the Holy Torah."

The Heavenly Court nodded in agreement. At that moment, Eliyahu HaNavi[25] came forward and said, "If Rabbi Eliezer must be tested, let me be the one to test him." The Heavenly Court agreed, and Eliyahu descended into this world.

The very next Shabbos afternoon, Rabbi Eliezer's guests were sitting at his dining room table after enjoying a sumptuous Shabbos meal, when

---

[23] Angel that serves as the Adversary.
[24] Righteous woman.
[25] Elijah the Prophet.

they heard a knock at the door. Rabbi Eliezer opened the door to a man in torn, dirty clothing.

The beggar carried a walking stick and a sack over his shoulder — a clear desecration of the Holy Shabbos, when carrying is not permitted. After muttering "Guht Shabbos," the beggar barged in, dropped his sack and walking stick by the door, and sat down at the Shabbos table.

Rabbi Eliezer showed no sign of annoyance that this newest arrival appeared to be desecrating the Holy Shabbos. Instead, while Rebbetzyn Sarah prepared another place at the table, Rabbi Eliezer brought him wine for Kiddush and two loaves of bread for HaMotzi.[26] The beggar mumbled unintelligible blessings over the wine and bread, and began to wolf down the food.

Rabbi Eliezer's other guests were shocked and dismayed at the behavior of the new arrival. Carrying a walking stick and a sack is a clear desecration of the Shabbos. To eat and drink with barely a mumbled blessing — incorrect at that — especially at the house of Rabbi Eliezer, was an outrage. They all watched Rabbi Eliezer to see how he would react. But he showed no sign of displeasure, as he served his new guest.

---

[26] Blessing over bread.

A number of the guests began to harass Reb Eliezer about being so kind to the beggar that had just arrived (Eliyahu HaNavi) and who was clearly breaking Shabbos. It reached a point where Reb Eliezer got so upset that he went to another room and was crying. There he realized that while he was feeling upset, the guest must also be feeling embarrassed, so he went back and gave the new guest extra attention. He also gave extra attention to this guest during the third meal of Shabbos.

That night, during the celebration of Melavah Malka, Rabbi Eliezer continued to personally serve the beggar, while telling stories of the Holy Rabbis.

The next morning, when the beggar was preparing to depart, Rabbi Eliezer gave him a donation and blessed him to have great success in all matters — family, health, and livelihood. As was his custom, Rabbi Eliezer escorted the beggar to the door and accompanied him outside to the front of the house.

It was then that the beggar revealed himself. "I am Eliyahu HaNavi and I have been sent to test you. You passed the challenge during Shabbos and because of your selfless love and your acceptance of others, you are worthy of having a son who will guide all of the Congregation of Israel and bring an infusion of G•dly light to the world!"

Within a year, the blessing was fulfilled, and a cherished son named Yisrael was born to Rabbi Eliezer and Rebbetzyn Sarah. Later, Yisrael attained renown as the holy Baal Shem Tov. May his merits protect us!

And so it was.

The Baal Shem Tov taught it is a good practice for the physical man to rejoice on the Sabbath. Through this, the spiritual form can enjoy its attachment to G•d all the more.

SHABBOS JOY

THE Baal Shem Tov called together his inner circle of disciples, the Chevrayah Kadisha, and announced, "Next Shabbos, I'm going to show you what Shabbos really is." The disciples were so excited they could barely wait for the next Shabbos to arrive.

Finally, the day came. They carefully prepared themselves by immersing themselves in the mikveh, dressing in their special Shabbos clothes, and coming early to the synagogue on Friday afternoon — long before the Shabbos evening prayers were to be recited. When the Kabbalas Shabbos prayers started, they prayed next to the Baal Shem Tov, but didn't see anything out of the ordinary.

Just before the Shabbos evening prayers were to end, they noticed the Baal Shem Tov staring towards one side of the synagogue. When they looked in that direction, all they noticed was a poor, simple Jewish man praying intensely and with great joy. Still, it wasn't such an unusual sight at the Baal Shem Tov's synagogue to see someone praying like that. And other than the way he was praying, they didn't notice anything special about the man.

After the prayers, the Baal Shem Tov motioned for his close followers to join him in his study. They sat around a table next to the window. Because it was summer and the windows were open, they could see the man who had been praying with such fervor during the Shabbos evening prayers enter his rundown house and could even hear him greet his wife.

"Good Shabbos, my sweet wife," he said, joyously.

"And a restful and holy Shabbos to you, my dearest husband," she responded.

The Baal Shem Tov's followers could hear the husband singing Shalom Aleichem. When he finished, he said to his wife, "Sweetheart, let's make Kiddush."

But the couple was so poor, they had no money for wine. So the wife placed two small rolls of bread on the Shabbos table and said, "My dear husband, we have no wine. Please make Kiddush over these two rolls."

"That's fine," he replied, "I'm sure the rolls will taste as delicious as the most special wine." They washed their hands with a blessing, said HaMotzi,[27] and shared the two rolls of bread.

Then the wife spoke. "For the fish course, I've made something special." She got up and brought a platter of beans to the Shabbos table.

She placed a spoonful of beans on each of their plates and said, "May it be G•d's will that these beans have the taste of a wonderful fish delicacy."

As they ate the beans, their faces shone with delight.

The husband sang a few traditional Shabbos songs and then said, "Thank G•d we have everything we need to celebrate the holy Shabbos. Let's have the soup course now."

They both took another spoonful of beans and smiled. "Umm, what a wonderful Shabbos soup," they remarked to each other.

Then she served a third spoonful of beans to take the place of the traditional meat dish and a fourth spoonful as a dessert.

"Come, my sweet wife, let us dance to celebrate the holy Shabbos." So they both got up and

---

[27] The blessing over bread.

began to dance about their Shabbos table and laughed and laughed.

Each of the disciples standing with the Baal Shem Tov felt a warm glow rise within themselves. The Baal Shem Tov whispered, "You are each experiencing Shabbos joy, similar to the joy this holy couple has been feeling. You should realize that it is not the simple food that they tasted, but the Shabbos itself."

And so it was.

CHAPTER TWO

ROSH HASHANAH

L'CHAYIM — TO LIFE!

REB Feivel was a simple Jew. He had a little farm in the Polish countryside and lived a meager life with his wife and four children. But he had a dream. From the minute he heard about the Baal Shem Tov, he longed to see him. For years he saved and scrimped until finally this year he had enough for the journey and to hold his family till he returned.

The weather smelled of winter. It was the Jewish month of Elul, the month of 'Teshuvah'.[28] Then the month of Tishrei with Rosh Hashanah, Yom Kippur, Succos, and Simchas Torah would follow. Hundreds, even thousands of Chassidim would be there together; learning, praying, hearing the words of the Holy Baal Shem Tov, and seeing his holy face. He couldn't wait!

After a five day journey, cramped in a wagon with ten other Chassidim, he finally arrived in the town of Mezibush, the home of the Baal Shem Tov.

---

[28] Repentance; literally turning back to G•d.

What he had heard was exactly right. Even the air was different here; it seemed to be shouting, 'Rosh HaShanah is coming! The King of the Universe is near!'

He was so excited! Everyone was heading into the shule and he followed, suitcase in hand. In another minute he would see him. He would see the Baal Shem Tov in person!

But he was in for a big surprise.

The shule was packed with hundreds of excited Chassidim talking, saying prayers and learning Torah. Suddenly everyone became silent; the Rebbe was entering!

The Baal Shem appeared from a side door, gave a quick penetrating look around the room and suddenly fixed his eyes on Reb Feivel!

Feivel was in awe. This was the moment he had been waiting for. But why was the Rebbe staring at him? Everything was dreamlike; he vaguely felt that he was the center of attention, but all he saw was the master's piercing eyes looking deeply into his very being.

Unexpectedly, the Baal Shem Tov lowered his head in deep thought, or perhaps prayer. Then he looked up once again and called out: "Reb Feivel, Reb Feivel! Fool! What are you doing here?"

The silence was deafening, the Chassidim were afraid to breathe. Something very strange was going on; something was clearly wrong.

"Aren't you ashamed of yourself?" exclaimed the Baal Shem Tov. "How dare you come into a holy place like this!"

Feivel was confused, his head was spinning, he tried to move but there was nowhere to go.

"Leave!" shouted the Baal Shem Tov, "leave here immediately!"

He started moving backwards, afraid to turn his back on the holy man but afraid to stay even another second, his heart was pounding and his whole body started to a sweat.

When he finally stumbled outside onto the street, he was crying and disorientated. Still in a daze, he walked right over to the carriage stand, paid for the five day journey home, climbed in and was on his way back while still in a stupor.

After a few hours, the wagon stopped in front of an inn. "What's this?" he asked the driver. "Why are we stopping?"

"We can't travel at night! So we'll stay here at the inn."

Poor Feivel was so bewildered by his encounter with the Baal Shem Tov, he didn't notice anything. He got out of the carriage still clutching his old suitcase and dragged himself into the inn.

Trying to understand what had happened, he sat at table in a corner, ordered a beer and went over the events of the day. Maybe he did do some sort of sin . . . maybe it was a punishment. He realized that he didn't learn much Torah, but that couldn't be the reason the Baal Shem Tov was so angry with him. After all, everyone knew that above everything else, the Baal Shem Tov loved every Jew, even unlearned ones.

While still deep in thought, he was disturbed by the sound of another carriage stopping, and then joyous singing from outside. It got louder and louder until the inn door opened and a group of Chassidim came pouring in. Knowing that they were only hours away from seeing the Baal Shem Tov, they were feeling good and in high spirits.

"Give us a few bottles of vodka," several said in unison, "tomorrow we'll be with the Rebbe!"

"Oy!" groaned poor Feivel bitterly, "Oy, oy, the Rebbe!" And he began to weep quietly to himself.

Feivel quietly sat in the shadows, watching the Chassidim push a few tables together, sitting down, and pouring vodka for one another, toasting l'chayim, saying words of Torah and singing.

The effect of all this joy was to make Feivel more depressed. Suddenly, he felt two of the Chassidim lift him to his feet and pull him over to their table.

He tried to resist and begged them to leave him alone, but to no avail. They had decided that he must be one of the Misnagdim (opposers of the Baal Shem Tov) – why else such a long face? They had agreed upon seeing Feivel that they had a religious duty to transform him.

So they forced him to drink and say l'chayim with them. It wasn't long before Feivel joined in with the singing and dancing, the hours passed like minutes.

"And then they heard a rooster crow — it is already dawn!'

After putting on their tallis and tefillin and davening the morning's prayer, the Chassidim got back into their carriage along with a very drunk Feivel still clutching his old suitcase, shouting, "We're going to the Rebbe for Yom Tov!" and began another song.

Five hours later, they arrived in Mezibush and were on their way to the Baal Shem Tov's shule. Two of them had their arms under Feivel's and were 'carrying' him with them.

When they finally put him down, they were in the Baal Shem Tov's shule. Feivel, still somewhat dazed, realized he was just where the Baal Shem Tov had yelled at him to leave less than 24 hours ago.

Suddenly the room fell silent, the side door opened, and the Baal Shem Tov entered the shule. Almost immediately, he looked towards Feivel. At the instant their eyes met, Feivel felt as though a bucket of freezing water had been thrown on him.

He froze in place, and became white from embarrassment. He wanted to run from the shule, but it was as if he was glued to the floor.

"Welcome, Reb Feivel" shouted out the Baal Shem Tov. "My beloved Reb Feivel, where have you been? I've been very worried about you."

Feivel was completely mixed up. "What's going on?" he thought. "Maybe yesterday never happened, or maybe now I'm dreaming!" Just then the Baal Shem Tov beckoned him to come over. The Chassidim moved aside making a path for him.

The Baal Shem Tov took Feivel's hand and explained, "My dear Reb Feivel, you didn't know it but yesterday when you entered this shule, the Angel of Death entered with you. I instantly realized that you wouldn't live to see Rosh Hashanah.

"I prayed for mercy but to no avail; it had been decreed in Heaven that your time to leave this world had come. I knew I had to do something quickly. It is known that embarrassing someone in public is like killing him, so I yelled harsh words at you with the idea that making you feel deeply ashamed of yourself would cause the Heavenly decree to be withdrawn. But I knew it hadn't worked when I saw the Angel of Death dancing over your head.

"So another idea popped into my mind. I thought that if I told you to leave, you'd probably immediately take the first carriage back to your home. Since it is a five day journey, I knew you would stop at the nearest inn for the night. Being so agitated, I assumed you'd probably stay awake, sitting at one of the tables and drinking all night.

"Now I reasoned to myself, many groups of Chassidim on their way here also aren't able to travel at night and would have to stop at that same inn. Being so excited about coming here, they also won't be able to sleep because they'd be too happy and seeing someone sad, they would probably try to cheer you up by making you sit with them and share their vodka. As we all know, when the Chassidim drink vodka they don't just make a blessing, they say 'L'Chayim' which means 'To Life!'

"Now according to the Torah Reb Feivel, when three observant Jews sit together, they have the power of a court. So when they all raised their cups to you and declared: 'To Life!' this was like a legal decision for life that overrode the power of the previous Heavenly decree.

"And, thank G•d it worked: the Angel of Death has departed. Welcome to Mezibush!"

And so it was.

THE SECRET OF THE SHOFAR

"In the seventh month, on the first day of the month, there shall be a rest day for you, a remembrance with shofar blasts, a holy convocation." *Leviticus 23:24*

"You shall sound a broken blast on the shofar . . ." *Leviticus 25:9*

AND then there was the time that the Baal Shem Tov summoned one of his close disciples, Reb Wolf Kitzes. "Reb Wolf, would you honor us with blowing the shofar in shule this year on Rosh Hashanah?"

"Of course Rebbe, even though I do not feel qualified for such a holy task," Reb Wolf immediately answered. "If you could instruct me on what I should I meditate on while I'm blowing the different blasts of the shofar, I would be most grateful."

For the following two weeks before the day of Rosh Hashanah arrived, the Baal Shem Tov instructed Reb Wolf on the kavanos — the mystical significance of the Divine Names associated with each of the blasts — that he should meditate on while blowing the shofar. Reb Wolf began practicing blowing the shofar, and studied intently the kavanos that the Baal Shem Tov had taught him.

To be certain he would not forget, he wrote down the kavanos on a piece of paper so that he could glance at them while blowing the shofar.

The Baal Shem noticed Reb Wolf writing kavanos down, and spoke to him about it. "Reb Wolf, do you really have to write out the kavanos? It is not wise to write down such secrets, and besides, I am sure you'll remember them when the time comes."

But Reb Wolf was nervous, so he finished writing them on a small piece of paper that he carefully placed in his pocket.

On the first day of Rosh Hashanah, as Reb Wolf made his way to shule, a sudden gust of wind blew the note from his pocket.

When the time came for the sounding of the shofar, Reb Wolf carefully removed his shofar from its velvet bag and walked to the bimah. As he reached into his pocket, he froze in horror! The piece of paper with the kavanos was gone! Reb Wolf frantically searched his pockets but the note was nowhere to be found.

The whole congregation stood ready to hear the holy sounds of the shofar. Reb Wolf was a nervous wreck! But he had no choice but to start blowing.

At this highest moment in the Rosh Hashanah prayer service, all stared in anticipation at Reb Wolf as he placed the shofar to his lips. He tried as hard as he could to remember, but could not recall one single intention that he had studied so diligently.

He was so upset. "Not only did I stupidly loose the note with the kavanos, but I can't even remember a single one!" Reb Wolf was broken hearted and he began to weep. With a broken heart and tears streaming down his cheeks, he blew the shofar the best he could.

When the prayers had ended, the Baal Shem Tov approached Reb Wolf and said: "In the King's palace, there are many doors and each requires its own special key. But there is a way that one can open all of the doors and that is with an ax. The mystical kavanos that you so intently studied are the keys to each of the different gates to the Heavenly palace, where each gate requires its own specific kavanah. But a broken and humbled heart can break open all of the gates. My dear Reb Wolf, this is what you accomplished with your blowing of the shofar."

And so it was.

CHAPTER THREE

SHABBOS TESHUVAH

SHABBOS TESHUVAH

"YISRAEL, Yisrael! Whatever is the matter?" The rebbetzyn sounded very alarmed. She had been awakened from her regular Shabbos after-dinner nap by her husband's cries. In a moment, she was by the side of his bed shouting his name. With that, the Baal Shem Tov sat up with a start and then sighed with relief.

"Thank G•d you woke me up now, my dear Chanala. Had you delayed a moment more I would not have awoken at all!"

"What do you mean, Yisrael," she gasped, why did you cry out so in your sleep?"

"I'll explain. But first call the Chevraya Kaddisha to come here, I also want to tell them what just happened to me."

The year was 1755. The day was Shabbos Teshuvah,[29] and the time, as already mentioned, was after the morning davening and the afternoon Shabbos meal.

---

[29] Repentance; literally turning back to G•d.

It did not take long for the the Baal Shem Tov's close followers to gather in his study. He began his strange tale.

"Every Shabbos, when I recite the silent Mussaf prayer, my soul ascends to the Heavenly worlds above. There I listen to what is being learned in the Yeshiva Above and I later transmit some of these Torah secrets to you, my dearest Chassidim, at the shalosh seudos table.

"I have for several years yearned to see a very close friend who already passed on to the World of Truth, the great Tzaddik, Reb Nachman Kassover. Each time I sought him, I was not able to locate him. I tried various combinations of prayers and holy incantations to find his resting place in the world of souls until it was finally revealed to me how to realize my desire.

"Today I recited the required prayers, concentrated upon the necessary holy thoughts and finally found my soul soaring to heavenly realms that I had never visited before. I saw buildings shimmering of pure gold; palaces of dazzling diamond before my eyes; sapphire spires adorning the high and spacious houses of study which were all around me. The sound of Torah was heard in these hundreds of study houses and I entered several to see what they were like. The groups of souls within each shone like angels, each one occupied with his own special aspect of Torah, be it Gemorra, Aggadata, Mishnah or Chumash. I looked about and was awed.

"To whom belongs this glory?" I asked. "Who is your leader here?"

"Our Torah study pays homage to the chosen of G•d, Reb Nachman of Kassover," came an answer from a chorus of the souls.

"And where is his resting place? May I see it?" I asked in awe.

"Someone grasped my hand and led me to Reb Nachman's beis medrash. Reb Nachman himself appeared as fire. His countenance shone like an angel's. His brilliance illuminated the far reaches of that unending Heavenly realm. It was an awe inspiring sight which left me stunned for several minutes. I gazed upon him, dressed all in white, his tallis over his head, and asked, 'Who are all these souls I see around me?'

"My dear brother," he answered me, "the souls you see belong to people whom I showed the path of righteousness in my lifetime on earth. Some of them were righteous men who had transgressed while others were incorrigible evildoers whom I was able to admonish by gentle words until they finally repented and began walking the paths of righteousness. It is these souls who praise and extol the living G•d, Blessed be He.

"'Dear brother,' he went on to say, "do you desire to remain here with me? You can, you know. All you need do is relinquish your soul to the angel you are acquainted with. Your body will then remain on earth below and you can stay here near me. You will not even have to experience the pangs of death or be confronted by the Angel of Death. Here, I and other Tzaddikim will take you and show you your eternal resting place. Isn't this what you truly want? The decision is yours; it is in your hands.'

"I vacillated. It was a tremendous decision to make. One main objection came to the fore; I desired to be buried in Eretz Yisrael, for a soul buried in the Holy Land ascends higher than one buried outside its holy boundaries.

"'Your fate is to be buried in your own land and not in the Holy Land,' Reb Nachman revealed to me. 'I am not at liberty to disclose the reason why. But if you agree to remain here with me, I will be able to reveal to you many, many things.'

"Again I vacillated, torn in opposite directions. My thoughts turned to those whom I would leave behind. Could I depart my loved ones, my worthy Rebbetzyn, my dear son and daughter, and my eminent talmidim? Could I leave them without a last will and testament, without guidelines for the future? Could I suddenly expire like an empty person? I decided I could not. One must prepare for one's death and not just leave on a whim. I made my painful decision and informed Reb Nachman. But he would not acquiesce. He argued, begged, cajoled until I could stand it no longer and emitted a loud yell at the thought of leaving behind my loved ones and disciples.

"This was the shout which woke my Rebbetzyn and made her awaken me in turn. And thank G•d she did, for it was just in time. I could not have withstood the conflict for much longer. She succeeded in returning my soul to its rightful place in my body."

And so it was.

CHAPTER FOUR

YOM KIPPUR

COCK-A-DOODLE-DO!

AND then there was the time that in a small village near the holy community of Mezibush (the home of the Baal Shem Tov), there lived a simple boy. He had only received a basic Jewish education and could barely read the "aleph bais".[30] He had left cheder[31] at a young age to help his father care for the small farm they leased from the local Poritz. The boy cared for the few animals they had — one old cow and a few chickens.

The boy had one strange skill: He could sing to his chickens as he went about his chores in the chicken-coop, and the chickens would always lay an abundance of eggs — more than any other chickens on the surrounding farms. Everyone who passed by could hear him saying, "Cock-a-doodle-do."[32]

When the boy reached the age of twelve, his father said: "My son, you are old enough to go with me to Mezibush for the high holidays, and to pray

---

[30] The Hebrew alphabet.
[31] Hebrew school for young Jewish boys.
[32] Cook-re-koo as pronounced on Yiddish.

at the shule of the holy Rabbi Yisrael Baal Shem Tov."

Several days before Yom Kippur, the father and his son embarked on their journey with a group traveling from their village to Mezibush. They arrived in Mezibush just in time to settle in at the local inn, immerse in the mikveh and rush to the Baal Shem Tov's shule for Kol Nidrei.

The shule was packed. People stood in silent thought, the men in their white kittels[33] and talleisim, and the women in their finest clothes. The boy was deeply affected by the solemnity of the scene. All stood in preparation for the holy Day of Judgment when the fate of each person is decided for the following year. Each person sought forgiveness for past transgressions and to be inscribed in the Book of Life for a year of abundant health, happiness, and sustenance for themselves and their families.

The father and son stood shoulder to shoulder in the crowded shule. The boy stared into his machzor,[34] but could hardly read a word. He stood watching the chazzan lead the prayers as tears

---

[33] White robe worn on certain holidays and for burial.
[34] Holiday prayer book.

streamed down his cheeks. All around him, people stood with their eyes closed in prayer.

As the sky darkened and the Kol Nidrei prayer was intoned, the Baal Shem Tov realized that there was a judgment in Heaven against the Jewish community. Throughout that night, and the whole next day, the Baal Shem Tov stood in deep prayer and meditation. The boy felt that something was wrong. The Chassidim gathered about in grave concern as their Rebbe stood motionless at his shtender.[35] Word had spread that something was amiss, and people began to weep with a feeling of dread.

The boy turned to his father and asked, "Why is everyone so upset and worried?" But his father only answered with, "Shah! We are all praying that G•d should have mercy on us!"

The boy couldn't take it! Suddenly, without thinking, he took a deep breath and burst out as loudly as he could, "Cock-a-doodle-do! G•d have mercy on us!"

The entire congregation was horrified! The men yelled angrily, "Keep quiet you fool!" and the women mumbled among themselves. Somebody asked the boy to leave the shule, but he refused,

---

[35] Prayer stand to hold prayer book.

saying, "I am a Jew too! Where should I go on Yom Kippur?"

At that moment, the Baal Shem Tov stirred. He stepped back three steps indicating the completion of his silent prayer, and began to sing a joyful melody. Finally, the shofar blew and the holy day of Yom Kippur ended. The Baal Shem Tov's face was radiant. As he walked from the shule wishing everyone well, he paused in front of the young boy and nodded with a broad, warm smile.

That night, as he sat at the festive meal with his close followers, the Baal Shem Tov spoke of a grave threat that hung over the Jewish community from the moment Yom Kippur began. "I tried my best to intercede, but the Heavenly Court would not hear my arguments. But then, just as the sentence was about to be sealed, a strange sound rang out throughout the Heavens: 'Cock-a-doodle-do! G•d have mercy on us!' The Heavenly Court was so pleased with this prayer that came from the depths of a simple Jewish soul that thank G•d, the decree against our community was annulled."

And so it was.

A MODERN DAY BAAL SHEM TOV STORY

When "perestroika"[36] became a reality in the former Soviet Union, Jews after many decades of forced assimilation were finally able to live openly as Jews again. The next year, in 1987, a young Chabad Rabbi, sent by the Rabbi Menachem Mendel Schneerson, the seventh Lubavitcher Rebbe, was leading the services in the main synagogue of Kiev on Yom Kippur night.

Announcements of the Yom Kippur services had been posted all over Kiev and Jews responded eagerly. Old men who remembered accompanying their parents to shule as children, young families who wanted a taste of their heritage after more than a half century of Soviet persecution, and youth in their teens who barely knew they were Jewish, flocked to the main synagogue.

The services began with the chazzan chanting Kol Nidrei. The moving melody stirred the hearts of all those who had come. But as the service proceeded, the Chabad Rabbi sensed feelings of disap-

---

[36] The policy of economic and governmental reform instituted by Mikhail Gorbachev in the Soviet Union during the mid-1980s.

pointment beginning to surface. After all, most of the people had never before even been in a synagogue nor knew how to pray together with the chazzan. Despite the best intentions, Hebrew — Russian prayer books, and his explanations in Russian, the Chabad Rabbi could sense that the people were becoming bored, and within their hearts a question was beginning to take form: "Were these the prayers that they had yearned for so many years to be allowed to say?"

In the middle of the services, after the silent Amidah prayer, the young Rabbi decided to make one more attempt to strengthen their involvement in the proceedings. So he ascended to the lectern and began to tell them the following Baal Shem Tov story:

One Yom Kippur, the holy Baal Shem Tov was praying together with his students in a small Polish village. Through his spiritual vision, he detected that harsh, heavenly judgments had been decreed against the Jewish people. He and his students tried with all the strength they could muster to cry out to G•d and implore Him to rescind these decrees and grant the Jews a year of blessing.

This deep feeling took hold of all the inhabitants of the village and everyone began praying with a deep heart-felt prayer.

Among the inhabitants of the village was a simple shepherd boy. He did not know how to read or even follow from the Hebrew prayer book; indeed, he could just barely read the letters of the alef-bais. As the intensity of feeling in the synagogue began to mount, he decided that he also wanted to pray. But he did not know how. He could not read the words of the prayer book or mimic the prayers of the other congregants.

So he opened the prayer book to the first page and began to recite the letters: alef, bais, vais — reading the entire Hebrew alphabet. Then he called out: "G•d, this is all I can do. You know how the prayers should be pronounced. Please, arrange the letters in the proper way."

This simple, genuine prayer resounded powerfully within the Heavenly Court and the harsh decrees were rescinded and the Jews were granted blessings and good fortune for the following year.

The Chabad Rabbi paused for a moment to let the story impact his listeners. Suddenly a voice in the shule called out, "alef" and thousands of voices thundered back "alef." The voice continued: "bais," and the thousands responded "bais." They continued to pronounce every letter in the Hebrew alphabet.

And then they began to file out of the synagogue. They had recited their prayers.

And so it was.

CHAPTER FIVE

SUCCOS

A DRY SUCCAH

"During these seven days you must live in Succahs. This is so that future generations will know that I (G•d) had the Israelites live in Succahs when I brought them out of Egypt." *Leviticus 23:42-43*

ONE year, in the holy community of Kitov, it poured with rain on the first night of Succos. Rabbi Chaim, a great Torah scholar and opponent to the fledgling Chassidic movement ("the Sect"), was slightly aggravated that he would be unable to enjoy the first night in the Succah.[37]

While waiting in his house for the rain to abate, Reb Chaim saw one of his acquaintances casually walking down the street as if he had already finished his Yom Tov meal in the Succah. When Rabbi Chaim inquired as to where he was going, the man told him that he was returning from having dinner in the Succah of Rabbi Gershon Kitover.[38]

---

[37] Thatched hut covered with schach [typically branches or bamboo] so that the stars are visible.

[38] The brother-in-law and close follower of the Baal Shem Tov.

"And Rabbi Chaim," he continued, "there was a miracle there because not a single drop of rain was falling through the schach."

Rabbi Chaim asked his son to go to Rabbi Gershon's Succah and see if it was true that it wasn't raining in there. When his son came to the Rabbi Gershon's Succah, he looked in and sure enough, everyone was sitting, talking and eating. There was not a single drop of rain coming through the schach into the Succah. Rabbi Gershon invited Rabbi Chaim's son to join them but he refused, explaining that he had to return to have Yom Tov dinner with his father.

When the son returned, he told his father that what he had heard was true. "Father, Rabbi Gershon was sitting in his Succah, and I saw with my own eyes that there was not even a single drop of rain coming into the Succah."

Rabbi Chaim rolled his eyes. Of course he believed his son's report but he wasn't that impressed. The rain finally relented and Rabbi Chaim and his son went into their own wet Succah for Kiddush and the Yom Tov meal. Naturally, they discussed the miracle of Rabbi Gershon's dry Succah and other miracles that the so-called Tzaddikim of the Sect were able to do.

Rabbi Chaim remarked, "In my opinion, creating such miracles, as obviously done by our friend Rabbi Gershon, is against the spirit of the Torah."

Early the next morning, Rabbi Chaim and Rabbi Gershon met on their way to the mikveh, in preparation for fulfilling the mitzvah of the lulav and esrog.

"Rabbi," said Rabbi Gershon to Rabbi Chaim, "I understand that you were sitting in your Succah last night and speaking loshon hara[39] about me."

Rabbi Chaim answered with astonishment, "How did you find out about what I said in my Succah? I was sitting there completely alone except for my son. And I'm sure he didn't tell you what I said. The only logical answer is that a Heavenly angel told you. But that seems impossible because an angel does not have the authority to speak loshon hara."

Rabbi Gershon answered, "Our Sages teach us that 'Whoever fulfills one mitzvah acquires one angel to speak up in his defense, and whoever does one transgression acquires one prosecuting angel to speak against him.' So it was that prosecuting angel

---

[39] Slander.

who you created last night by your loshon hara about me who came and told me what you said."

And so it was.

THE SUCCAH OF REB PINCHAS OF KORETZ

Although every holiday is considered joyous, Succos is specifically called The "Season of our Rejoicing". True joy is the pleasure one Jew has when he shares with his fellow Jew. *Divrei Chassidim*

REB Pinchas of Koretz was a disciple of the Baal Shem Tov and known as a Tzaddik and a great masmid.[40] He was a reserved, quiet man, and spoke little other than what was necessary in the course of his Torah study.

With time, people began to approach him for blessings and spiritual advice. Being that his blessings were very effective, his reputation began to spread, and soon there was a steady stream of people seeking his help. But Reb Pinchas became increasingly more upset at the number of people at his door asking for his blessing and felt it was taking too much time away from his Torah study. He finally became so aggravated by the number of interruptions of people seeking his blessings, that

---

[40] Devoted totally to the study of Torah.

63

he prayed, "Dear G•d, please make people hate me so they won't seek me out and disturb my study of Torah."

The Talmud states that "the words of the Tzaddik has a power" and so the heartfelt prayer from such a holy man did not go unheeded.

Soon, people began to become indifferent to Reb Pinchas, and the number of those knocking on his door began to decrease. It wasn't long before no one visited at all.

Reb Pinchas was quite pleased with his new freedom. He was able to totally immerse himself in his Torah studies without interruption.

And so it was until the holy festival of Succos approached when Reb Pinchas' wife tried to arrange as always to have someone build their Succah so not to disturb her husband's studying. But that year, there was such lack of interest in Reb Pinchas that no one was available to help. Finally, exhausting all avenues, she was forced to hire a non-Jew to help her, and the Succah was completed with just minutes to spare before the holiday began.

On the first night of Succos, Reb Pinchas sat in his Succah eating his holiday meal and studying Torah. As the hour grew late, his Rebbetzyn went to bed and Reb Pinchas sat alone in his Succah bent over his holy books.

Suddenly he heard a knock and looked up to see an old, Holy man standing at the door of his Succah. The man had a flowing white beard and was dressed in a long white robe. Reb Pinchas realized this was not a normal person but a Heavenly being standing at the door of his Succah.

Each night of Succos, we recite the "Ushpizin" — inviting each of our forefathers as guests, to our Succah. As it was the first night of the festival, Reb Pinchas realized that it was the first guest, Avraham Avienu[41] who was standing before him.

"Baruch Haba!"[42] exclaimed Reb Pinchas jumping to his feet, "welcome to my humble Succah".

Avraham Aveinu smiled and replied, "Thank you Reb Pinchas, but I am sorry, I only visit those Succahs in which the joy of the holy festival of Succos can be felt. But since you have no guests your joy is lacking." And with that, he disappeared.

Reb Pinchas was devastated and immediately realized the grave error he had made in praying that he be left alone. So he again prayed to G•d for forgiveness, and from that day on, Reb Pinchas

---

[41] Our father Abraham, the Patriarch.
[42] Blessed to those who come.

always lent a ready ear and gave abundant blessings to anyone that approached him.

And so it was.

CHAPTER SIX

SIMCHAS TORAH

THE EXCHANGE

DURING the Simchas Torah festivities in the Baal Shem Tov's shule, the Chassidim got so carried away with fervent dancing and drinking, that they were transported to other worlds. Even one such experience in the Baal Shem Tov's shule was cherished for a lifetime.

On one particular year, the joy was more pronounced than ever before. The Chassidim danced in a circle carrying the Torahs hour after hour. They actually felt the presence of the Shechinah in their midst.

After several hours, one of the Chassidim, Reb Yaakov, had to stop dancing because his shoe tore apart. He was miserable. It was just not the same looking on as being within the circle of Chassidim. Besides being his only pair of shoes, he was well aware that he would not be able to afford a new pair of shoes.

The Baal Shem Tov's daughter Adel noticed Reb Yaakov sitting at the side of the room, saw his torn shoes, and understood the situation. She went over to Reb Yaakov and he said in Polish, "If you get me shoes, I promise you'll have a child." While such a promise would not normally be easily given,

69

the Chassidim close to the Baal Shem Tov possessed powers similar to those of their Rebbe.

The Baal Shem Tov heard Reb Yaakov's promise and said to Adel, "Quick get him the shoes."

She went searching for shoes but couldn't find any. So, she took off her shoes and gave them to him.

Reb Yaakov said, "You gave me two shoes and you'll have two children."

Then he put the shoes on and lost no time in joining his friends.

By the following year, Boruch, the Baal Shem Tov's grandson, was born to Adel and her husband Yechiel Mechiel Ashkenazi. Later, Reb Moshe Ephriam was born to them.

And so it was.

THE CANOPY OF FIRE

IT was Simchas Torah at the synagogue of the Baal Shem Tov. After the evening Yom Tov prayers, the Chassidim left the synagogue to eat the special Yom Tov dinner and then returned to join their Rebbe in the festivities. They gathered in the study hall of the synagogue and danced and whirled and twirled around in a circle for many hours while they passed the Sefer Torahs from one to another, sang the traditional Simchas Torah songs, and drank lots of wine.

By early morning, the faithful were feeling very b'simchah[43] and some even a little shicher.[44] They begged the shammos[45] to bring up more wine from the Baal Shem Tov's wine cellar.

When Rebbetzyn Chana, the Baal Shem Tov's wife, heard the commotion from the study hall and the Chassidim pleading with the shammos to bring up more wine from the wine cellar, she became worried that there wouldn't be enough wine left for making the blessing over Kiddush and Havdalah.

---

[43] Joyful.
[44] Drunk.
[45] Caretaker of the shule.

So she quickly went into the private study of her husband, the Baal Shem Tov, and requested of him, "Yisrael, go into the study hall and tell your Chassidim to stop drinking and dancing because we won't have enough wine for making Kiddush and Havdalah."

The Baal Shem Tov chuckled and said, "Chana, I agree. Would you please tell them to stop and go home?"

She immediately went to the study hall to give the Chassidim the message from her husband, the Rebbe. But when she entered the hall, she saw them still dancing in a circle with flames of fire burning above their heads in the shape of a circular canopy. She immediately collected the empty wine containers scattered around the hall, went down to the wine cellar to refill them, and brought them back to the dancing Chassidim.

A while later, the Baal Shem Tov inquired, "So Chana, did you tell them to go home?"

Chana answered, "Next time, Yisrael, it might be better if you tell them yourself."

And so it was.

CHAPTER SEVEN

TU'BSHVAT

THE ORANGE ORCHARD

AND then there was the time one winter when the Baal Shem Tov was traveling in Russia with one of his great disciples, Rabbi Moshe Shoham of Dulina. Since the Russian countryside was covered with snow at that time, they were traveling in a sleigh driven by Alexei, the Baal Shem Tov's wagon driver.

When Tu B'Shvat[46] arrived, they found themselves in the countryside, far away from any town. They were very disappointed that they didn't have a fruit[47] with which to celebrate the holiday.

The Baal Shem Tov told Alexei to drive the sleigh off the main road and into one of the adjoining fields. After travelling a short distance, they came upon a field that not only was not snow-covered, but had an orchard of oranges. And most astounding was that not only wasn't it cold, but the climate was tropical!

---

[46] A holiday occurring on the 15th of Shvat celebrating the New Year of the trees.
[47] The custom is to eat from the seven species for which the Land of Israel is praised: ... a land of wheat and barley and (grape) vines and fig trees and pomegranates, a land of olive trees and (date) honey *(Deut. 8:8)*.

They immediately picked some of the oranges, and joyfully made the blessings to celebrate the holiday.

Rabbi Moshe Shoham also took a few oranges back to the sleigh for later.

All this time, Reb Moshe did not even wonder how an orange orchard with a tropical climate appeared suddenly in the Russian countryside in the middle of winter when in fact, oranges do not even grow in Russia during the summer. Being often around the Baal Shem Tov, he was so used to miracles that such events did not even cause him to wonder about such an awesome sight!

As they made their way back in the sleigh across the fields, Reb Moshe suddenly felt regret that he had not taken more oranges.

When they got back to the main road, for one reason or another, the Baal Shem Tov decided to rest briefly and Reb Moshe took the opportunity to return to the orchard. He followed the path of the sleigh tracks back, but when he reached the field, the orchard was gone and it was covered with snow. He quickly returned to the sleigh and to his surprise, the few oranges he had picked and had put in the sleigh had also disappeared.

When he asked the Baal Shem Tov about this, the latter responded, "When I felt unhappy

about having no fruit and not being able to celebrate Tu B'Shvat, I transported by mystical means
an orchard from the Land of Israel to that nearby
field. But since I brought the orchard solely to
perform a mitzvah, and not for our personal benefit,
the orchard and the few fruits you had taken disappeared afterward."

And so it was.

CHAPTER EIGHT

CHANUKAH

THE CHANUKAH LIGHTS

THE Baal Shem Tov had a special custom when the month of Kislev arrived. In the evening, he would gather together the children from the local cheder, including his own grandchildren, and tell them the story of the miracle of Chanukah. And to their delight, he would also help the children construct a new menorah each year.

They made a base, eight branches with cups to serve as vessels for the oil, two decorative lions with their red tongues extended, and a kind of hollow finger on the right side for the shammos, the "servant" candle used to light the other candles. This design was later known as the Baal Shem Tov's menorah.

The Chassidim said that the menorah constructed by the Baal Shem Tov and the children looked like the menorah in the Second Temple which never fell into Roman hands when they destroyed the Temple. It is said that this menorah ascended into heaven and when the holy Messiah comes, will return back to earth and light the path for the redeemed.

On the first night of Chanukah, when the first candle was to be lit, this special menorah built by the Baal Shem Tov and the children was placed in the study hall of the Baal Shem Tov's shule. Many Chassidim travelled great distances to be in the company of the Baal Shem Tov when the menorah was lit.

The Baal Shem Tov always taught Torah before lighting the candle. One year when all the Chassidim were packed into the study hall, he taught the following as soon as the evening prayers were completed.

"The verse says: 'When you light — literally, 'elevate' — the candles.' Why does it say: 'When you elevate'? It is because someone who lights the Chanukah candles must also light himself and someone who elevates the candles must also elevate himself to the level of self-sacrifice."

Then the Baal Shem Tov's face began to shine with fervor and he asked, "Is everyone ready for self-sacrifice, like that of the Maccabees — Matisyahu and his sons?"

All the Chassidim together with the children who had constructed the menorah, answered in one voice, "We're ready!"

Then they started to sing a niggun and to dance — and as they sang and danced pouring out their very souls, it seemed to them that they were lifted up in flames above the ground on which they danced. The Baal Shem Tov danced with them, hand holding hand, shoulder against shoulder. Every once in a while, a certain Chassid jumped up on the shoulders of his friends and loudly called out the "Shema" (Hear O Yisrael, the L•rd our G•d, the L•rd is One)!"

Before the Baal Shem Tov lit the candle, he gazed fixedly at the congregation and at the Chassid who had been calling out the Shema. Then, after meditating with closed eyes for a long while, he opened his eyes and said, "Why do we draw out the final syllable of the word echad (Hebrew for one) when we chant the Shema? It is because the essence of everything is the One — the One above and the One below; without the 'One' there's no Shema."

And the Chassidim, who were listening to this teaching with their eyes closed absorbed it fully, and their feeling of brotherhood and of oneness, immediately increased and was strengthened, because they understood that the essence of Chassidism is the "One."

As usual, the chorus of singers began a new niggun for chanting the Shema for that year. The Chassidim used to say that whoever has not heard the yearly melody for the Shema sung in the beis medrash of the Baal Shem Tov has never truly heard a niggun in his whole life.

The Baal Shem Tov continued by teaching about the parts of the menorah, beginning with the base on which rested the eight branches with their eight cups to hold the pure oil, in which the oil-saturated wicks floated, to be lit.

He said, "The power of the branches is in their all having one foundation, one base, which unites them and brings them to the level of holiness. Although each wick burns in its own cup — yet, because they all have a common base, it's as if they're all a single branch. And that's the reason we make only one blessing for the candle lighting, saying, 'Blessed are You, O L•rd our G•d ... who has commanded us to light the candle of Chanukah' — because all the eight candles are like one candle that's completely holy."

Suddenly, a voice broke the silence, the voice of a grandson of an elderly villager named Reb Pinchas, one of the foremost Chassidim. This little boy called out, "What about the shammos, Rebbe?" The boy's voice rose up, as if from the hearts of all the children there, for they were all wondering why the Baal Shem Tov had not yet taught about the "servant candle." Even the Chassidim and those in the Baal Shem Tov's inner circle, who were startled by the cry that disturbed the silence, opened their eyes wide, expectantly wondering what the Baal Shem Tov would say.

He stood there quietly for a little while, then looked tenderly at the child — who was himself surprised by his own voice and question — and said, "The holiness of the shammos is not less than that of the other candles. In fact, it even has an extra degree of holiness because one is permitted to use its light, which is different from the other candles whose light one is not permitted to use for any purpose, but only to view. And that is the special merit of the 'hewers of wood and the drawers of water' among the Jewish people. That thanks to their help and supplies, the kohanim could offer up the sacrifices on the altar in the Temple."

Then, turning to the little boy who had called out the question, the Baal Shem Tov added, "and you, boychik'l, may G•d grant that you have the merit to be one of the holy servants, one of the shammosim, who bring the redemption!"

And so it was.

CHAPTER NINE

PURIM

A SWEET SONG

THE true meaning of Purim joy was best experienced in the company of the saintly Rabbi Yisrael Baal Shem Tov. While there was not much of the Purim feast in the way of food or drink to go around, there was an nonstop flow of Torah from the Baal Shem Tov. It was an amazing experience which forever remained imprinted in the minds and hearts of those fortunate enough to have experienced this occasion.

One year, Rabbi Meir Margolis, a faithful follower of the Baal Shem Tov, brought with him his five year old son, Shaul. Besides being a bright little boy with a sharp mind, Shaul had a very sweet voice. During the Purim feast which took place in the Study Hall, the Baal Shem Tov unexpectedly placed Shaul next to him and asked him to sing.

Being that it was Purim, Shaul sang in his sweetest voice Shoshanas Yaakov, the prayer said after reading the Megillah on Purim. This song was about "the Lily of Jacob (the Jewish people) which rejoiced and was glad, when all saw Mordechai in purple clad, because G•d has been Israel's salvation and hope in every generation . . ."

When Purim was over and Rabbi Meir was preparing to go home, the Baal Shem Tov said to him, "I know you have to return to Lemberg to take care of your community, but I would like you to leave your son Shaul with me for a few days. After Shabbos, please G•d, I will personally bring him home."

Rabbi Meir Margolis was very happy that the saintly Baal Shem Tov took such a great liking to his young son, and he knew within himself that there must be a good reason for the Baal Shem Tov wanting Shaul to stay with him for Shabbos. But at the same time, he wasn't sure that Shaul, being so young, would be willing to stay.

When asked if he wanted to stay with the Rebbe, Shaul immediately replied, "Yes Father, I want to stay and I promise that I will not cry."

After Shaul's father left, the Baal Shem Tov spent time teaching little Shaul Chumash as he had long ago taught the little children when he had been an assistant schoolteacher.

On the morning after Shabbos, the Baal Shem Tov asked Alexei, his driver, to prepare his sleigh, as they were going on a trip to Lemberg. He sat little Shaul next to him on the sleigh, and took two other young men from among his close students to accompany them. There was still snow on the road, and the sleigh glided swiftly along. After travelling some distance, they passed an inn from which came the sound of drunken voices. The local peasants were drinking heavily and having a rousing good time.

Without notice, the Baal Shem Tov told Alexei to turn the sleigh around and stop at the inn. His students were very surprised. Why would the Rebbe want to be in the company of drunken peasants? Surely they would be passing other, more suitable inns on the way! But in respect to their Rebbe, they said nothing. When they arrived, they all got out of the sleigh and followed the Rebbe into the inn.

Holding little Shaul by the hand, the Baal Shem Tov stood for a few moments among the noisy peasants. Then he clapped his hands to get their attention. "SILENCE!" he called out in Polish which the Baal Shem Tov knew well.

Immediately there was silence, and all turned to look at the visitors whom they had not noticed before.

"Do you want to hear real singing?" the Baal Shem Tov called out to them. Without waiting for their answer, he added: "Listen to this boy and you will know what real singing is!"

Then he turned to Shaul and said to him, "Shaul, sing Shoshanas Yaakov."

Shaul, even though he was quite young, felt that there was something special about all this, and he sang with much feeling. He sang as he had never sung before.

The peasants listened with captivated attention, and tears streamed down their faces. When Shaul finished they remained spellbound for a moment, and then all of them suddenly burst out, "Bravo! Bravo! Wonderful!"

The Baal Shem Tov raised his hand, and all became quiet again. He turned to face three young peasant children who were about Shaul's age, and he beckoned them to come over.

"What is your name?" he asked one of them.

"Ivan!" replied the boy, a little frightened.

"And yours?" he asked the second boy.

"Mine is Stephan," replied the boy.

"And yours?"

"Gregan!" replied the third boy.

"Now, boys," said the Baal Shem Tov, "meet little Shaul, who sang for you. Do you like him?"

"Oh, yes!" they replied eagerly.

"Well, then," said the Baal Shem Tov. "Remember, just as you feel friendly to little Shaul now, you should always be friendly to him. Remember that!"

"Yes, Rabbi, we will," the boys promised.

The Baal Shem Tov and his party then said goodbye and departed as suddenly as they had appeared.

The peasants in the inn were left speechless at the sudden appearance and disappearance of the holy man and his followers. Even the Baal Shem Tov's students were greatly puzzled by their Rabbi's strange conduct. Of course, they assumed there must have been an important reason for stopping at the inn, but they could not even imagine what reason was.

Many years passed. By now, Reb Shaul Margolis was a respected Talmud scholar and a successful merchant.

It was the Fast of Esther and Reb Shaul was hurrying home from a business trip. He wanted to be on time to hear the Megillah at the onset of Purim that evening, and he drove his horses as fast as they would go. He was also anxious to get out of the dark forest through which he was passing. Suddenly he was forced to stop when three, murderous looking bandits jumped out of the thick woods, armed with knives and hatchets.

While two bandits seized him and tied him to a tree, the third grabbed the bag in which Reb Shaul was carrying a large sum of money.

"We are going to kill you," the bandits said.

Shaul pleaded with the bandits to give him a few minutes to say his last prayers to the Almighty.

"Pray all you want," they said, "your G•d cannot help you now."

Reb Shaul said vidui (the last prayer before returning one's soul to his Maker), while the bandits were counting the money and dividing it among themselves.

His eyes were closed and filled with tears. A vision of his wife and children arose before him. They would be waiting for his return, to celebrate Purim with him, yet he would not be there. He always used to read the Megillah for them at home, in case they missed a single word of it in the synagogue, and then he would sing for them Shoshanas Yaakov, as he had once sung it for the holy Baal Shem Tov. The mere thought of this joyous Purim prayer made Shaul feel better. Yes, if he had to die, he wanted to die with Shoshanas Yaakov on his lips.

Reb Shaul sang with all his heart and soul, the same way he had sung in the inn for the drunken peasants when he was a little boy.

"The Lily of Jacob rejoiced and was glad when all saw Mordechai in purple clad. You, O G•d, have been Israel's salvation and their hope in every generation . . ."

When he finished, he closed his eyes while expecting a death blow at any moment, but all was quiet. When he opened his eyes, the three bandits were standing before him, open-mouthed in wonder, as the peasants had stood long ago in the inn. He looked again and suddenly it occurred to him that he knew who they were.

"Aren't you Ivan?" Shaul cried out to the first man. "And you're Stephan and your name is Gregan?"

As he spoke, he could see that the bandits had also recognized him. Gone was the fierce look on their faces, and in its place there was sheer wonder and, yes, friendliness.

The men then returned all of Reb Shaul's possessions and escorted him out of the forest. This was all part of a vision that the Baal Shem Tov had foreseen many years before. Just as on Purim of long ago when everything suddenly turned around to save the Jewish people, here also everything mysteriously turned around to save Reb Shaul's life.

And so it was.

CHAPTER TEN

SHABBOS HAGADOL

THE DANCING BEAR

IT was Shabbos HaGadol[48] in Mezibush, the city where Rabbi Yisrael Baal Shem Tov resided. The entire Jewish community was worried. They heard whisperings from the local peasants that a non-Jewish baby had been killed so that its blood could be put into the Passover matzos. The allegation that Jews murdered non-Jews to obtain blood for the Passover matzos, known as a blood libel, was used since early times to persecute Jews. They had also learned that a certain judge was spreading the rumor, "The baby was probably killed by their shochet."

In the synagogue of Rabbi Yisrael Baal Shem Tov, a large gathering of his Chassidim gathered to daven. In the middle of davening the Shabbos morning prayers, the Baal Shem Tov removed his Tallis and stepped outside from the synagogue. Everyone waited for the Rebbe to return so they could continue with the Torah reading and remainder of the Sabbath prayers. After a long time had

---

[48] The Shabbos right before Passover commemorating how G•d.

99

passed, some Chassidim went outside to see if something was wrong.

Just then, they saw a group of village boys running down the street following after a huge, dancing, brown bear being led with a rope by a gypsy. The Chassidim were surprised to see the Baal Shem Tov among the group of boys following the bear. They too joined in and followed the bear to see what was going to happen. "After all," they thought, "the Rebbe doesn't usually leave prayers to run after a bear."

The gypsy stopped in front of the judge's house and had the bear perform a number of tricks. The bear caught a ball, stood on its two hind legs and even danced. Suddenly, the bear broke loose from the rope and started to act in a crazy way. Everyone in the crowd began to run away, afraid that the bear might turn on them. But the Baal Shem Tov remained there by the bear. Just then, the bear broke into the front door of the judge's house. Many, including the Baal Shem Tov, excitedly ran to the windows to see what the bear was going to do in the house.

They watched with amazement as the bear deliberately moved a table and pulled up the floor boards under the table as if they were match sticks. Then, the bear began to dig into the ground until it uncovered a baby buried in the earth. Later it was discovered that the dead baby was an illegitimate child of a local, non-Jewish villager. The bear picked up the dead child and waved it around for all to see.

The Baal Shem Tov yelled out, "You are all witnesses of this attempted blood libel. The judge accused us of killing a child to use the blood for the Matzos. In fact, the dead child is buried here in this house."

Then, the Baal Shem Tov returned to the synagogue to complete his Sabbath prayers.

And so it was.

CHAPTER ELEVEN

PASSOVER

PAASOVER IN ISTANBUL

AND it once happened that ten days before Pesach, the Baal Shem Tov and his daughter Adel arrived in Istanbul on their way to Eretz Yisrael (Land of Israel). They had sailed from the port city of Odessa leaving ample time to reach Eretz Yisrael before the holiday began. Once out to sea, the weather turned stormy. After a day of treacherous weather, the captain announced, "Unless the weather subsides by daybreak, we will dock in Istanbul to wait for better weather. It is too dangerous to continue."

Now, just two days before Passover, the Baal Shem Tov and his daughter Adel found themselves in Istanbul. They were exhausted and penniless after the hardship of the arduous journey from Mezibush.

Usually, the Baal Shem Tov's reputation preceded him wherever he went. But In Istanbul, no one recognized the famous Rebbe as he walked among the Jewish people busy with their Passover preparations.

Yet another strange event had occurred; the Baal Shem Tov suddenly lost all of his Heavenly powers.

Not knowing where to spend Passover, the Baal Shem Tov went to the local beis medrash hoping that someone would invite him and his daughter to their home to celebrate the Passover Seder.

Meanwhile, Adel took her father's holiday clothing down to the sea to wash. She sat by a rock, weeping as she scrubbed, remembering the beautiful Seders at her home in Mezibush and thinking of their prospects for Pesach, without wine, matzos or other kosher food.

As Adel sat weeping, a passenger ship arrived at the harbor. Among the passengers was a wealthy merchant who had noticed the weeping young girl. Touched by her sorrowful appearance, he approached to offer some assistance.

Adel was not one to talk to about personal issues with strangers, and particularly regarding her father, but in her emotional state she broke down. "My father is a famous Tzaddik who is being punished by Heaven by having all his powers taken from him. We are alone in Istanbul with no food, and nowhere to celebrate the Yom Tov."

"Please don't worry my child," said the merchant, "I'll send a carriage to bring you and your father to my home where you can both spend the Yom Tov in comfort."

Adel hurried to the beis medrash to tell her father the good news. Together, they were taken by carriage to the merchant's luxurious home where they were made to feel welcome. After refreshing themselves with food and drink, they were shown to their rooms. The Baal Shem Tov promptly went to sleep in anticipation of the evening Seder.

The Baal Shem Tov slept for the rest of the day. Meanwhile, his host went to shule for the evening prayers. Seeing that the Baal Shem Tov was still sleeping on his return, the merchant asked Adel to wake her father as the hour was late and certainly the time to start the Passover Seder.

"I'm very sorry," replied Adel, "but I cannot wake my father. Such a thing is disrespectful. Every act of a Tzaddik has deep meaning. If my father is sleeping, then it is for a purpose."

"Very well," responded the host, "I will have to wake him myself."

As the merchant entered the room and approached the bed, he was stunned by what he saw: The body of the Baal Shem Tov was glowing brightly and tears flowed from his closed eyes. The merchant immediately realized that his guest was no simple man so he quickly and quietly left the room. After what he had seen, he was not about to disturb the Tzaddik's rest.

A short while later, the Baal Shem Tov woke from his sleep thoroughly refreshed. While he had slept, his spiritual powers had returned and he began his evening prayers with his usual fervor and devotion, a sight which further inspired and impressed his host.

The Baal Shem Tov led the Seder with his great inspiration, singing, and expounding the inner meanings of the Exodus from Egypt. His host, the merchant, and Adel sat spellbound. When the Baal Shem Tov came to the words of the Hallel prayer, "Le'oseh niflaos — For He performs wonders," the Tzaddik's voice rang out loud and clear, as he articulated the words with utter devotion. The sound of his words carried out far into the stillness of the night. The rest of the Seder passed as before and it was early morning by the time they had finished.

Until now, the merchant had refrained from making any comments or asking questions for fear of disturbing his G•dly visitor. But now that the Seder was over, he ventured several comments.

"Rabbi, if I may ask, why did you sing that particular verse of the Hallel prayer so loudly?"

"The Jews of Istanbul were in grave danger," disclosed the Baal Shem Tov. "While I slept my soul ascended to Heaven where I interceded with all my might on their behalf. At the very moment that I sang the Hallel so loudly, I was informed that the Heavenly decree had been nullified. You will learn all about it tomorrow morning in shule."

On the following morning, as the congregation assembled for their holiday prayers, one prominent member of their community suddenly rushed in. "Mazel Tov, my good friends. Congratulate yourselves on having escaped imminent danger, praised be G•d." Everyone crowded around to hear the details of his surprising announcement.

The Story Told By The Prominent Congregant

"As you may well know," he began, "our late Sultan was in the habit of dressing in common clothing to walk incognito among his people, as did his father, the previous Sultan. This particular stroll took him far out of the city limits and before he realized what had happened, he was surrounded by a group of roving bandits. They seized him and brought him to their hideout. It occurred to the Sultan that these thieves did not know his identity.

"After his pockets had been emptied of the all his valuables, the Sultan was confident that he would be released. But the thieves informed him that they must kill him since he knew the location of their hideout.

"The Sultan contemplated his chances of survival. 'If I reveal my identity, they will surely kill me, for they would realize that capital punishment would await them if anyone knew whom they had captured and robbed. Let me use my wits instead and see if I cannot save myself.'

"'I am trained with a particular skill which may bring you much profit,' he told his captors. They gathered around the Sultan in interest: 'I know how to fashion valuable tapestries, given the proper raw materials. My products will fetch high prices for you on the market. Try and see.'

"The robbers were willing, for the sake of profit, to give his plan a fair try. They purchased simple mats from which the Sultan fashioned his tapestry. After two days, the first product was ready for the market.

"The finished product did not over impress the bandits but the Sultan hastened to warn, 'this tapestry can only be appreciated by a true connoisseur of art. Do not be daunted if at first people laugh at the price you ask. But by no means are you to settle for less than what I tell you. Go from shop to shop until you find the proper customer, a person who is expert enough to appreciate this work.'

"It happened just as the captive Sultan had foretold. At the first place he entered, the bandit was greeted by jeers and hoots when he demanded an outlandish price for his 'exquisite' tapestry. Everyone thought he was a crazy person. The scene was repeated at the next store and again at the next. By now a large crowd of people had gathered to see the outcome of the farce. Who would be mad enough, they wondered, to pay the price the man was asking for what appeared to be a simple mat?

Just then my father, who was a wine merchant, happened to walk by, attracted by the commotion. He learned from the people around me the cause of the gathering and pushed forward sensing something had happened. He was shown the tapestry and quoted the ridiculous price.

First he looked at the bandit's face and saw that he didn't look like a crazy person. That made him think that there was clearly something deeper than met the eye. So he asked the man if he could examine the tapestry closely. A quick look showed him that there was nothing especially artistic about the piece before him save for one letter intricately woven and hidden in the cloth.

"'I'll take it at your price,' my father told him, and then went on to ask about the craftsman who had fashioned it. The man was reluctant to give him any information. 'If you like this work, I can bring you more like it,' he promised but that was all he would say.

"The bandit returned to his hideout with good news for the imprisoned Sultan. Not only had his cloth been purchased at his price, but the customer wished to order more. The Sultan was certain that some clever person had caught on to his ruse and set about his work cheerfully, ingeniously weaving a second initial into the center of the cloth.

"When this cloth was brought to my father the next day, he immediately saw the second initial and knew that he had been right in assuming that it contained a clue. After paying the price, he sat with the tapestry thinking whose initials they were. Suddenly it struck him and he hurried to the Sultan's palace with his tale. The palace was in pandemonium. No one knew what had happened to the Sultan. Searches were being organized but no trace or clue had yet been found. When my father presented his story and evidence, all agreed it was indeed the Sultan who was trying to send a message as to his whereabouts. My father was told to hold his tongue but continue to purchase the tapestries as they were brought.

"Day after day, letter by letter, the Sultan spelled out directions to his location. Soon, a brigade of soldiers was dispatched to the robber's hideout where they succeeded in freeing the Sultan.

"The Sultan did not forget my father, his benefactor, and summoned him to the palace. 'How can I thank you enough?' he said. 'Name a reward and you will have it.'

"My father refused to hear of a reward. 'Is it not reward enough that I have had the privilege to save the life of my Sultan? It is a privilege which is a reward in itself.'

"This was not enough for the Sultan, however. He had a proclamation written stating that my father and his children would forever have the privilege of free access to the Sultan's palace and the attention of the Sultan himself for any need they might have. This all happened to my father many, many years ago. He never had any reason use his privilege.

"My father passed away as did the late Sultan. Until this day, I found no cause to seek access to the Sultan.

"This year, our Sultan happened to be walking through the market place with his Vizier, who is well known as one who vehemently hates Jews, when he noticed a flurry of activity. Cartloads of strange bread were being transported from place to place. The Sultan had never seen anything like it. 'What are these cakes?' he asked his Vizier.

"'These are called matzos,' the Vizier replied. 'They are eaten by the Jews throughout the holiday they call Passover. Some Jews pride themselves in eating only "shmura" (watched) matzos made from the blood of a Muslim child which they slaughter for that purpose.'

"The Sultan was stunned!

"'Don't take my word for it, Your Majesty,' the counselor said, 'make your own inquiries. You will hear the same story.'

"The Sultan did ask around and learned that there were, in fact, many Jews who only ate the special loaves known as shmura matzas which were baked under the most careful supervision and he inferred that his Vizier's comments had indeed been true. He was horrified.

"He instituted a special inquiry to determine which Jews ate only shmura matzah. He intended to have his guards arrest the culprits while they ate at their Seder, and imprison them.

"Then, last night, on the eve of our holiday, I had a dream. My father appeared to me to warn me of the impending danger. He instructed me to go straight to the Sultan by virtue of my special privilege of free entry and present the true version of the blood libel to acquit my fellow Jews. I was to expose the Vizier for what he was — not a devout Moslem as the Sultan thought, but a practicing Greek Orthodox Christian. 'Tell the Sultan to send his soldiers to the Vizier's home in the middle of the night,' my father instructed, 'and they will find him in bed with a cross upon his chest.'

"I awoke towards evening, deciding that the dream had been simply a dream, and I went about with my preparations for the evening Seder. But suddenly I became very tired — so much so I had to lie down. I fell asleep again and my father appeared once more, warning me to heed his advice for only I could save the community. When I awoke the second time, I realized that it was not a meaningless dream and that immediate action had to be taken.

"It was already late at night when I arrived at the Sultan's palace. Despite my right to enter the palace when I wished, I did not want to cause a commotion and wake the Sultan. I begged the palace guards to take me to the "Old Queen," the Sultan's mother.

"The Queen happened to be awake, and she listened patiently to my story. I hastened to remind her that in all these years neither my father not I had used our privilege. If I was asking her to intercede for the Jews on my behalf, it was because the matter was one of life or death.

"The Queen asked me to wait while she spoke to her son. She did not plan to present the Jew's cause for she had heard nothing of the impending decree and thought it might not be true. Instead, she decided to tell her son she had dreamed that his father, the late Sultan, had appeared to her in a dream, instructing her to warn her son against issuing any evil decrees.

"At first the young Sultan denied any impending evil decrees. But when his mother mentioned the Jews, he confessed. 'Yes, Mother, I did issue the decree. But my law concerning the Jews is a beneficial one for it concerns those Jews who use Moslem blood in their matzah baking. I have ordered this cult to be destroyed for the public benefit.'

"Seeing that the Jew had spoken the truth, the Queen now told the entire story to her son who asked that the wine merchant be brought before him. I ran forward, throwing myself at his feet, my story pouring out in tearful pleas. I begged the

Sultan to follow my father's suggestion of sending soldiers to surprise the Vizier in his own home to prove that he was unfaithful to the Moslem faith. The Sultan followed my suggestion and everything that I had predicted proved to be true. In their fury, the soldiers executed the Vizier on the spot.

"The Sultan immediately cancelled the decree that would have killed us all."

"All this happened, just at that time I was reciting the Hallel prayer, did it not?" the Baal Shem Tov asked the wine merchant. The statement was confirmed, for indeed, the Baal Shem Tov had become aware of the miracle at the very minute which coincided with his recital of "Le'ose niflaos gedolos (For he performs wonders)!"

And so it was.

HIS WIFE WAS RIGHT

AND then there was the time, when there was a feeling of worry in the holy community of Mezibush, the home of the holy Rabbi Yisrael ben Eliezer. It was the Passover of 1756, and as on all Jewish holidays, many of his followers came to Mezibush to spend Passover with their Rebbe. It was always an uplifting, almost magical experience to be in the presence of the Baal Shem Tov, especially at the time of a Jewish holiday.

On this Passover, the followers were upset because they could sense that something was terribly wrong with the Baal Shem Tov. He was not in his usual buoyant spirits.

After the search for chometz on the night before the Passover Seder, the Baal Shem Tov told ten of his closest disciples to say Tehillim with great concentration.

While saying this prayer, Reb Tzvi (the scribe of the Baal Shem Tov) came running and yelled, "L•rd of the Universe, the Rebbe fainted and fell onto the floor of his study." Everyone was upset, but no one would dare go into the study and disturb the Rebbe.

The next day before the Passover Seder, the Baal Shem Tov prayed the morning prayers in a despondent mood. When he finished his prayers, he expounded about 'Trust in G•d.' He explained that 'true and complete faith in G•d' can only occur when a person can't see any way to overcome their problem. And still at that very moment, the person believes without a doubt that G•d will save them from their problem. And most importantly, the person shows this trust and faith in G•d by being b'simchah (having a joyful attitude). Being b'simchah shows that the person has no doubt that soon, with G•d's help, they will overcome their problem.

As soon as the Baal Shem Tov finished this discourse, his mood noticeably changed. He seemed more at ease. The followers whispered among themselves, "The change in the Rebbe's mood is not because of a change in a spiritual decree about which he was no doubt concerned. No, it's because the Rebbe caused a change in his mood in order to remove a terrible Heavenly decree, G•d help us."

In the afternoon of that same day, when the time came to bake the matzos (matzos made just before the Seder are considered the most precious), the Baal Shem Tov went to the mikveh and then to bake the matzos. His mood had improved even more and he actually seemed to be joyous. That night, in the synagogue of the Baal Shem Tov, the special evening prayers for Passover were chanted with great enthusiasm.

After the prayers, his close disciples were invited to the Baal Shem Tov's Seder. The disciples sat around the Seder table eagerly awaiting to hear the Rebbe's insights on the Haggadah. But this Passover night was different than others because the Baal Shem Tov did not expound on the deep mystical meanings of the Haggadah. Instead, he just quietly read the text. The disciples were disappointed.

Near the end of the Seder, the Baal Shem Tov closed his eyes. The disciples looked at each other thinking, "Is he in a state of deep meditation or did he 'almost' fall asleep?" they wondered. The room was silent. Suddenly, the Baal Shem Tov started laughing so hard that he could barely sit still in his chair.

"Mazel Tov!" he exclaimed, "thanks to G•d who has chosen the Torah, Moses our teacher and Yisrael. You should know that even the simplest Jew has the power to change a Heavenly edict."

The disciples sat speechless as he began to explain, "Yesterday morning, a terrible edict was decreed in Heaven against the Jews of a nearby village. The non-Jewish peasants in that village were planning to attack the Jews on the first night of the Passover."

"I prayed with all my strength, and I even had you help me. But we couldn't overcome the Heavenly decree. I finally gave up and put my trust in G•d that the decree would be rescinded. Right then I started to feel joyful. When we sat down to the Seder, the hour for the execution of the decree had arrived. I didn't see any hope for those Jews living in that village. But in a single instant, thank G•d, everything changed.

"During that time, a childless couple that are among my followers and lived in the village where the decree was to be executed, were sitting at their Seder table. Although they were simple, unlearned Jews, they were exceptionally kind, devout and full of good deeds. When they reached the section of the Haggadah about the Egyptians throwing the new born baby boys into the Nile, the wife started to cry. Her husband tried to comfort her, 'My sweet wife, don't be sad, after all the Jewish people were finally taken out of Egypt.'

"The wife spoke back, 'If G•d had blessed me with a son, I would have protected him and not let anyone hurt him. And I certainly would not have let anyone treat my son the way G•d let us be treated by the Egyptians.'

"The husband stood up for G•d saying, 'G•d is righteous in all that He does, it's only that we can't see or understand why it is good for us.'

"But the wife answered back, 'Why isn't G•d more compassionate? How could He have treated us like that? Even if we do sin, we are still His children.'

"And so the argument went back and forth as they worked their way through the Haggadah."

The Baal Shem Tov continued, "During this time, the case against the Jews of their village was being argued before the Heavenly Court. The defending angels were more persuasive when the wife presented her arguments and the accusing angels were more persuasive when the husband presented his rebuttals. I really couldn't tell what the outcome would be.

"Finally, after completing the fourth cup of wine near the end of the Seder, the husband couldn't think of another answer to his wife's arguments against G•d's behavior. So he conceded, 'My wife, you're right. G•d should have treated his children better.'

"They started to laugh, got up and began to dance around the Seder table. And at that very moment, the decree in Heaven against the Jews of their village was canceled," the Baal Shem Tov concluded.

The disciples were mesmerized with the story. Then, the Baal Shem Tov told them to place their hands on the shoulders of the person sitting on either side. When the Baal Shem Tov placed his hands on the shoulders of the person sitting on either side, the circle was closed and the disciples all saw a vision of the husband and wife dancing together around their Seder table celebrating the liberation of the Jewish people from Egypt. The Baal Shem Tov said with a little chuckle, "They should only know that they are also celebrating the liberation of the Jewish people of their own village."

And so it was.

CHAPTER TWELVE

SEVENTH DAY
OF PASSOVER

In the Torah reading (*Exodus 13:17 to 15:26*), we read that following the departure of the Jewish people from Egypt, Pharaoh regretted his decision to allow them to leave, and pursued them to the Reed Sea. There, Moshe raised his staff and the Sea split and the B'nei Yisrael crossed over. Once all of the B'nei Yisrael had crossed, Moshe again stretched out his staff and the water returned to its former state, drowning the pursuing Egyptians. When the B'nei Yisrael saw the dead Egyptians on the sea shore . . . . . "The people . . . . . believed in G•d and Moses His servant." *Exodus 14:31*

PERFECT FAITH

AND then there was the time that Rabbi Dovid Leikes, one of the Chevrayah Kadisha (inner circle of followers of the Baal Shem Tov), was speaking with several followers of his son-in-law, Reb Mottel of Chernobyl (also known as the Chernobyler Rebbe). Reb Dovid asked the followers of Reb Mottel, "Tell me. Do you have perfect faith in your Rebbe, Reb Mottel?"

None of the men responded.

After a pause Reb Dovid persisted, "So nu?"

Finally, one of Reb Mottel's adherents came back with, "Who can say he has perfect faith?"

Reb Dovid nodded and continued. "My friends, let me tell you a story about faith. Once, several of us in the Chevrayah Kadisha spent a Shabbos at an inn with the Rebbe. As usual, Seudah Shlishit went late into the night.

"The Baal Shem Tov told us of the mystical insights he had received while meditating, praying, and studying Torah during that Shabbos. When he finished speaking, we Benched, said Maariv and then Havdalah.

"Immediately afterwards," Reb Dovid continued, "we sat down together with the Baal Shem Tov for Melava Malkah.

"After a few minutes, the Baal Shem Tov turned to me and said, 'Reb Dovid, reach into your pocket and take out a gulden, please, and buy us some mead (honey wine) from the inn keeper.'

"I was still wearing my Shabbos clothes and of course I never carry money on Shabbos. Yet, without thought or hesitation, I reached into my pocket to take out the gulden, as my Rebbe had requested. And the most amazing thing! I found a gulden in my pocket."

The disciples of Reb Mottel, after hearing this story, commented to Reb Dovid, "You know, that is really not that amazing. It's just another miracle story about the Baal Shem Tov."

"Yes, that is so," said Reb Dovid, "but the point of my telling you the story is not to show that the Baal Shem Tov does miracles. My point is that my faith in my Rebbe, the Baal Shem Tov, was so great that I didn't even think to question his request. I just reached into my pocket for the money. That it was there was secondary."

And so it was.

CHAPTER THIRTEEN

LAG B'OMER

THE LAG B'OMER PARADE

AND then there was the time that the town where the Baal Shem Tov (before he was revealed as a holy man) was living received word that a gang of violent Cossacks were on their way to overrun the town and plunder or destroy whatever Jewish property they could get their hands on.

The elders of the Jewish community decided to abandon their homes and hide in the hills for a few days, until the invading Cossacks would leave. The Baal Shem Tov, still unknown as a holy man accompanied them. The people took refuge in the numerous caves that dotted the rugged terrain of the surrounding hills.

It was the holy day of Lag b'Omer. . . .

From their lookout places within the caves, they could see the gang of Cossacks ride through out their town. Unable to find any Jews to physically assault, they vented their anger and frustration on Jewish property. They found a large supply of whiskey and drank themselves into an inebriated state. And then the invaders broke into and ransack the Jewish homes and stores, taking piles of stolen valuables. If that wasn't enough, they set fire to a number of stores and houses.

Meanwhile, the Jews staying carefully hidden in the caves, all trembled in fear that the Cossacks would search the hills and discover their hiding places.

The Jews were startled to see that the barely known "Yisraelik" (a nickname for "Yisrael" the Baal Shem Tov's name) was assembling groups of their children outside of the caves, in broad daylight!

They begged him to stop but the Baal Shem Tov explained to them that it was the holy day of Lag B'Omer, a day to be outside in the fields, joyously celebrating the holiday commemorating the Yahrtzeit of Rabbi Shimon Bar Yochai, the author of the Zohar. He assured them that not only would the children not be endangered, but that the merit of their observance of Lag b'Omer would help protect and rescue the entire community.

Somehow his enthusiasm and confidence calmed the nervous parents, and they gave their permission.

While many of the parents were still worried, the Baal Shem Tov started a parade and the children marched along singing happily. At first, they were a bit afraid and sang only in low voices, but in only a few minutes their fear melted away as they raised their voices to join in the many cheerful tunes honoring Rabbi Shimon Bar Yochai.

As the parents watched their children with affection, they were drawn to the sight of the Baal Shem Tov. It was as if they had never seen him before. His face was aflame with joy as he sang and danced with the circle of children. The simple Yisraelik had suddenly been transformed into a holy man. His voice joined with those of the innocent children so that the singing sounded like that of Heavenly angels.

The parade and the singing continued for a long time. Afterwards, the Baal Shem Tov led the children to a small plateau, sat them on the grass, and gave to each of them cakes and cookies that he had brought with him. While they were eating, he told them stories about Rabbi Shimon bar Yochai and Rabbi Akiva. The children listened carefully and felt the powerful love that the Baal Shem Tov had for each of them.

The parents and the other adults from the village were still worried. How could Yisraelik keep their children so long in the open? They looked back and forth from the smoke and destruction in the village below and the children seated in front of the Baal Shem Tov.

Suddenly, they saw the Cossack gang run from the village in every direction. They left so suddenly that they didn't stop to take any of the stolen property with them. At first the Jews were afraid that the Cossacks were searching for them but the speed with which they disappeared calmed their fear. Soon after the Cossacks left, all the Jews returned to their village. The danger was over!

The Jews happily returned to their homes, amazed by the miracle that had taken place for them. They knew without doubt that the miracle occurred in the merit of their children's joyous celebration of the sage Rabbi Shimon Bar Yochai on the day of his Yartzeit — Lag B'Omer — with the man named Yisraelik.

Afterwards, they learned that the Cossacks were frightened away by a troop of government soldiers approaching the village.

Later that same day Yisraelik disappeared never to be seen by them again, at least as a simple Jew.

And so it was.

CHAPTER FOURTEEN

SHAVUOS

"There was thunder and lightning in the morning...
The people in the camp trembled. Moses led the
people out of the camp toward the Divine Presence."
Exodus 19:16,17

Experiencing the giving of the Torah, even for a
saint, is difficult.

A MATTER OF STRENGTH

AND then there was the time, just a few days
before the holy festival of Shavuos — the time of the
receiving of the holy Torah — when Reb Baruch of
Tuichin traveled to Mezibush to pray at the holy
resting place of his grandfather, the Baal Shem Tov.
Reb Baruch completed his prayers at the Baal
Shem Tov's gravesite, but he did not pay a visit to
his brother, Reb Moshe Chaim Ephraim of
Sudylkov. Instead, he returned home in time to
spend Shavuos with his Chassidim and his family.

Immediately after Shavuos, Reb Baruch again
traveled to pray at the grave of the Baal Shem Tov.
But this time, he stopped to visit his brother, Reb
Moshe Chaim Ephraim.

During their conversation, Reb Moshe Chaim Ephraim asked his brother: "Reb Baruch, when you came to our grandfather's holy gravesite before the festival, why did you not call on me? And why did you return again so soon after Yom Tov?"

Reb Baruch answered: "I was told from Above that if I so desired, I could receive the revelation of Torah on Shavuos with thunder and lightning, just as Moshe Rabbeinu (Moses our teacher) and the whole Jewish nation had received the Torah at Mt. Sinai. The lightning and thunder was a physical revelation of G•dliness that I wished to also experience."

"And so," he continued, "before Shavuos, I went to the graveside and asked our holy grandfather to intercede in Heaven so that I'd be granted the merit and the strength to receive the Torah in such a manner.

"When I returned to Tuichin, I did indeed receive the Torah on Shavuos with thunder and lightning. But afterwards, I did not have the strength to bear such a revelation, as each Jew has his own unique strengths and abilities, unlike any other individual. I thought my abilities would allow me to receive the Torah on the level of "lightning and thunder". But I now realize that such revelations are just too great for my nefesh (soul). My abilities and strengths are in other areas, where I can serve the Creator to the best of my abilities. One's desires should be in accordance with one's abilities and strength.

"So I returned and asked the Rebbe, our grandfather, to intercede again and have the revelation removed."

And so it was.

THE LAST REVELATION

ON the day of his passing from the world (the first day of Shavuos), the Baal Shem Tov was in his bed surrounded by his closest Chassidim. Only Reb Hershelah Tzvi, the Baal Shem Tov's son, was absent.

The Chassidim warily asked, "Rebbe, don't you want to give your son a few last instructions?"

The Baal Shem Tom answered with a sigh, "How can I? He is still sleeping."

A few Chassidim rushed out to wake Reb Hershelah. "Reb Hershelah, quick, wake up, your father the Rebbe is getting ready to leave the world."

"Oh no," answered Reb Hershelah with a shock, "that's impossible! I don't believe my father is passing on to the next world."

"Reb Hershelah," they said with a solemn voice, "the Rebbe said that he will leave the world today."

Reb Hershelah quickly dressed and rushed to his father's room. When he arrived at his father's side, Reb Hershelah started weeping, "Father, father, please don't leave us."

The Baal Shem Tov reached out and held his son's hand. "My dear son, I'm going to depart from this world. One thing I want you to know is that you have a very holy soul. When your mother and I conceived you, the very Heavens shook. At that time, I had the power to bring any soul I chose, even that of Adam HaRishon (the first man). But I selected your soul because it was very holy and possessed all that you will need."

"Please father, tell me something before you depart," begged Reb Hershelah.

So the Baal Shem Tov started to speak to his son, but his voice was barely audible.

"Father, I can't understand what you are trying to tell me," said Reb Hershelah in a distraught voice.

The Baal Shem Tov gathered his strength and spoke louder, "My dearest son, there is nothing that I can do now. Just listen and remember this Name."

Then the Baal Shem Tov motioned to his son to come closer. Reb Hershelah bent down very near to his father and the Baal Shem Tov whispered the Name to him. Then he said, "Whenever you concentrate on this Name, I will come and study with you."

Reb Hershelah spoke, "But what if I forget the Name?"

"Come close to me again," said the Baal Shem Tov, "and I'll tell you a way of remembering the Name."

After the Baal Shem Tov whispered the way to remember to Reb Hershelah, he closed his eyes and his soul ascended.

And to this day, no one knows the Name or how to remember the Name.

And so it was.

CHAPTER FIFTEEN

CHAI ELUL

THE SOUL OF THE BAAL SHEM TOV

AND then there was the time that the Tzaddik, Rabbi Adam Baal Shem, recounted that the soul of the Baal Shem Tov, was the gilgul (reincarnation) of a simple Jew who lived in Safed, Yisrael in the year 5333 (1573).

Once, this simple Jew had just completed Tikun Chatzos (midnight prayers for the destroyed Holy Temple), when he heard a knock on his door.

"Who's there?" he asked.

"It is Eliyahu Hanavi (Elijah the Prophet)."

He quickly opened the door and when Eliyahu entered, the room filled with light and joy.

"I have come to tell you the time of the coming of Moshiach and the Final Redemption. But first, you must tell me about the special deed you did on the day of your Bar Mitzvah. This deed has caused the Heavenly Court to rule that you are worthy of the revelation of the most esoteric of all secrets, the time of the Final Redemption and the coming of the Moshiach."

The simple Jew answered, "What I did was only for the glory of G•d and I will not reveal it to anyone. If this means that you won't tell me the secret of the time of the Final Redemption, then I'll have to forego that knowledge. I believe that a man's deeds should be solely for the glory of G•d."

Suddenly, Eliyahu disappeared and returned to Heaven. There, he found a great commotion caused by the man's loyalty to G•d, a loyalty which prevented him from learning one of the most important and deepest secrets of Heaven, the time of the coming of the Moshiach and the Final Redemption. The Heavenly Court then decided that Eliyahu HaNavi should nevertheless return and teach the simple Jew the depth and secrets of Torah.

This simple man was unique in his generation, but as he had wished, no one knew of his greatness. His deeds were solely for the glory of G•d.

When the time came for him to pass on to the Heavenly Worlds, his pure soul was brought before the Heavenly Court. It was ruled that his reward would be to return again to the earth and be reborn. This time he would be revealed to the world, and through him, a new way of life. He would purify the world with his spirit. This would glorify the Holy One Blessed be He, fill the earth with wisdom and thereby hasten the ultimate redemption and coming of Moshiach.

It was this selfsame soul of the simple Jew of Safed that was reborn in Rabbi Yisrael Baal Shem Tov on Chai Elul of 1698.

And so it was.

THE BIRTH OF RABBI SCHNEUR ZALMAN

AND then there was the time in a small shtetl in Poland, during the times of bloody pogroms and fierce anti-Semitism, that there lived what appeared to be a simple Jew by the name of Reb Boruch, and his wife, Rivka. Actually, Reb Boruch was a Tzaddik nistar (a hidden Saint) and one of the members of a group of Tzaddik nistars that included the Baal Shem Tov.

Reb Boruch and his wife Rivkah had been married for some years but had not been blessed with a child. At the prompting of his wife, Reb Boruch traveled many miles in the freezing, snowy winter to reach Mezibush and ask his Rebbe, the Baal Shem Tov, for a blessing. Without pause, the Baal Shem Tov blessed Reb Boruch and his wife that they merit to be blessed with a child, and added the words that the child "should reveal heavenly light hidden in this world."

Soon thereafter, Rivka became pregnant and on "Chai Elul" — the eighteenth day of the month of Elul, twelve days before Rosh Hashanah — the same birthday as that of the Holy Baal Shem Tov, Rivka gave birth to a baby boy whom they named Schneur Zalman. On that same day, the Baal Shem

Tov's close followers noted the particularly jubilant mood of their Rebbe. He led the daily prayers with deep kavanah, and afterwards a festive meal was held at which the Baal Shem Tov sang lively niggunim and even danced with unusual joy.

During the festive meal, the Baal Shem Tov said: "Today, a Neshamah Chadasha (a new soul that had not previously occupied a physical body) has come into the world. This soul will illuminate the world by spreading Torah and Chassidus[49] to sustain the spiritual well being of the Jewish people and will bring closer coming of the Moshiach."

After Yom Kippur, as is the tradition of Chassidim, Reb Boruch visited his Rebbe and requested a blessing for his newly born son. The Baal Shem Tov asked Reb Boruch to keep the news of the birth of his new son secret, and also gave specific instructions for the care and education of the child. In the following weeks, the Chassidim noted that the Baal Shem Tov mentioned the name Schneur Zalman three times during his Torah discourses.

The following year, Reb Boruch again returned to visit his Rebbe for the Yom Tov holidays. The Baal Shem Tov was very interested in the development of young Schneur Zalman, and asked

---

[49] Mystical explanations of the Torah.

Reb Boruch specific questions about the child. Again the Baal Shem Tov warned Reb Boruch not to talk to others about their son, particularly regarding his apparent intelligence — as is the nature of parents.

Again in the following year, Reb Boruch came to the Rebbe for Yom Tov and the Baal Shem Tov again asked many questions about the welfare of the child. Before departing for home, Reb Boruch told the Rebbe that G•d willing, on his next visit, when the child would turn three years old, he would bring his Schneur Zalman with him.

On the following Chai Elul, Reb Boruch brought young Schneur Zalman along with his mother Rivkah and his aunt Devorah Leah to the Baal Shem Tov to celebrate little Schneur Zalman's Upscherinish.[50] The Baal Shem Tov appeared very pleased at the joyous event. He cut some of the boy's locks, and then placing his holy hand on the boy's head, blessed little Schneur Zalman with the words of the Birchas Kohanim (Priestly blessing).[51]

---

[50] The first cutting of a boy's hair at three years old.
[51] May the L•rd bless you and guard you; May the L•rd make His face shed light upon you and be gracious unto you; May the L•rd lift up His face unto you and give you peace.

During their visit, young Schneur Zalman asked his mother who was the "old" man that had been the first to cut his hair. His mother told him he was his Zaide (Jewish for grandfather and the term used by the Alter Rebbe when speaking of the Baal Shem Tov). Following the joyous event, the Baal Shem Tov asked the child's mother Rivkah and aunt Devorah Leah to return home and not to reveal the events of the day.

Later, on that day of Chai Elul, there was a special gathering of the Chassidim in celebration of the Baal Shem Tov's birthday. The Baal Shem Tov mentioned that the Torah tells us that at three years of age, Avraham Avinu[52] recognized that there was one G•d. The Baal Shem Tov continued, "There is a great Neshamah in Poland that today reached the age of three years old and has recognized the Creator. He too will undergo mesirus nefesh[53] to reveal a new teaching of the holy Torah that will touch the souls of all Jews."

At that time, there was a great Torah scholar named Rabbi Yissochar Dov of Kalbink. The Baal Shem Tov arranged for him to be young Schneur Zalman's teacher, but asked Reb Yissochar Dov not

[52] The Patriarch, the father Abraham.
[53] Great self sacrifice.

153

to tell Schneur Zalman that the Baal Shem Tov had sent him.

Under the watchful eye of the Baal Shem Tov, the young Schneur Zalman flourished in his studies. He later became one of the 'Chevraya Kadisha' (The Holy Brotherhood of disciples of the Baal Shem Tov and the Mezritcher Maggid), who spread the teachings of Chassidus through Eastern Europe. Later, he become known as The Alter Rebbe — the first Rebbe of the Chabad-Lubavitch.

And so it was.

CHAPTER SIXTEEN

BIRTHDAY

BIRTHDAY WITH ELIYAHU HANAVI

AS recounted by the Baal Shem Tov...

"I was in a small village on my sixteenth birthday, Chai Elul of 5474 (1714).

"The local innkeeper was a very simple Jew named Aaron Shlomo. He could barely say his prayers in Hebrew and certainly had no idea what the words meant. Still, he had a great fear of Heaven and when anything happened to him he would say in Yiddish, 'Blessed be He, and may He be blessed forever and ever.'

"The innkeeper's wife named Zlate Rivkah, was also a very humble woman and would always say, 'Blessed be his Holy Name.'

"On that day, I went out to a field to meditate in solitude. This was to fulfill the instructions given by our Holy Sages of old that on your birthday, you should spend time meditating alone. During my meditation, I recited Psalms and concentrated on the yichudim[54] of the Divine Names.

---

[54] "Yichudim" are a form of kabalistic meditation based on different permutations and combinations of the Divine Names and attributes of G•d.

"While deeply immersed in my meditation, I lost my sense of time and awareness of my surroundings.

"Suddenly, I beheld Elijah the Prophet. He was beaming with light and had a broad smile on his face.

"I was very amazed that I should merit a revelation of Elijah the Prophet while alone. Previously, when spending time with the Tzaddik Rabbi Meir, and also with other hidden Tzaddikim, I had the fortune to see Elijah the Prophet. But to be privileged to this while alone — this was the very first time and I was amazed.

"And this is what he said to me: 'You are struggling with great effort to focus your mind upon the Divine Names that are within the verses of Tehillim.[55] But Aaron Shlomo the innkeeper and his wife Zlate are both ignorant of the yichudim of the Divine Names that are caused by his recitation of "Blessed be He, and may He be blessed for ever and ever" and her recitation of "Blessed be his Holy Name." Yet their yichudim cause a spiritual effect throughout all the Upper Worlds far beyond the yichudim of the Divine Names by even the great Tzaddikim.

---

[55] The Psalms composed by King David.

"Then, Elijah the Prophet told me about the pleasure G•d takes from the praise and thanksgiving of the men, women and children that praise the Holy One Blessed be He — especially when the praise comes from simple people, and most specifically when it is done continually — for then they are continuously bonded with G•d, Blessed be He, with pure faith and sincerity of heart.

"From that time, on I took upon myself a path in the service of G•d to bring men, women and children to say words of praise to G•d. I would always ask them about their health, the health of their children and about their material welfare — and they would answer me with different words of praise for the Holy One, blessed be He — each one in his or her own way.

"For several years I did this myself until at one of the gatherings of the hidden Tzaddikim, they all accepted this path to publicize the service of love of a fellow Jew."

And so it was.

CHAPTER SEVENTEEN

MARRIAGE

THE WEDDING BLESSINGS

A Jewish innkeeper had hired a teenage boy and a teenage girl. The boy and the girl were both orphans. Over time, they developed special feelings for each other. The special feelings were apparent to everyone who saw them together. The innkeeper promised that he would help them to get married, after they had worked for him a few years longer.

One day, the boy saw the innkeeper's wife scream at the girl. When the innkeeper's wife struck the girl, the boy screamed at the woman, and even raised his hand to her. The innkeeper, hearing the screams, rushed to see what the commotion was about. As luck would have it, it was just at the moment that he arrived, that the servant boy raised his hand against the innkeeper's wife.

The innkeeper ran over and grabbed the boy's hand. Then he started screaming at both of the orphan servants. When the boy spoke up and tried to explain that the innkeeper's wife had hit the girl, the innkeeper grew even angrier. He told them to pack their bags and get out of his inn. As the young couple walked out into the bitterly cold Ukrainian winter, the innkeeper yelled, "And I never want to see your ugly faces again!"

163

The young couple used all of their savings to buy a rickety old sled and a tired old horse. They traveled from town to town, looking for a place to settle. But, no luck. After weeks of traveling in freezing temperatures across the Ukrainian countryside, they had no food, no money, and didn't know where to go.

The day came when they were so weak and tired that they gave up. The cold filled their famished bodies. They lay unconscious in the sled, which the starving horse continued to drag down the road.

Late in the afternoon, the horse stopped next to a small fire around which a group of the Baal Shem Tov's disciples sat. Earlier that morning, the Baal Shem Tov had told Alexei, his wagon driver, to prepare the sled for a trip. Then, he had invited a group of his closest followers to accompany him on his travels — to an undisclosed destination. The disciples loved to join their Rebbe on such mysterious and magical trips.

As was often the case, once the sled had left Mezibush, Alexei put down the reins, took a few sips from a bottle of whiskey, snuggled up under a heavy blanket, and went to sleep for the duration of the trip. The horse and sled seemed to fly through the air and traveled a great distance in a short period of time.

On this trip, and in this fashion, the Baal Shem Tov and his disciples had traveled from early morning until late afternoon. The disciples were desperately cold, and they had quietly discussed among themselves how much longer it would be before they reached an inn — where they could warm up, eat, and, hopefully, spend the night. All of a sudden, the Baal Shem Tov announced that they would stop and daven Mincha beside the road.

The disciples wanted to continue on to the nearest inn, but the Baal Shem Tov insisted that they stop right there. They were all freezing so they decided to build a fire to warm themselves.

The fire was already blazing when the disciples completed the afternoon prayers. Then, almost out of nowhere, they saw a small sled pulled by a haggard horse slowly approaching their fire. The sled was covered in a sheet of white frost.

When they looked closer, they saw a teenage boy and girl huddled together under a pile of blankets. Their eyes were open and they looked as though they were staring through the layer of frost that covered their faces.

The disciples rushed over and pulled the young couple from the sled. They wrapped the blankets around them and placed them on the ground next to the fire in hopes of being able to "thaw out" their already blue bodies. When they regained consciousness, the disciples helped them sip from cups of hot tea and brandy.

After recovering, the boy and girl told the Baal Shem Tov and his followers that their names were Shlomo and Rivka and that they worked for a Jewish innkeeper and had been planning to get married. Then they told of the events that had lead to their being nearly frozen in the sled.

When they had finished telling their story, the Baal Shem Tov said, "A young man and a young woman cannot travel together like this without being married. We are going to make a chasana."[56] Without further discussion, they all got back into their sleds and started traveling.

Within a few hours, the two sleds had arrived at an inn. When the innkeeper heard the sounds of their arrival, he rushed out to greet the group of Chassidim. As he was instructing them regarding where they should put the sleds and bed down and feed the horses, he noticed Shlomo and Rivka.

"What are they doing here? They will not step foot in my inn!" he shouted.

---

[56] A wedding.

The innkeeper's wife, hearing her husband's yelling, came outside and stood next to her husband. "Get away from here, you dirty little brats," she screamed.

"Please," said the Baal Shem Tov, "we want to have a chasana at your inn."

"And who are the chosson[57] and the kallah,[58] may I ask?" queried the innkeeper.

"Why, it's this young couple," answered the Baal Shem Tov.

The innkeeper and his wife began to laugh uproariously. Then, the innkeeper suddenly became serious and said, "They will get married here — over my dead body."

The Baal Shem Tov took the innkeeper aside and spoke to him in a quiet voice. As the two men walked into the inn, the disciples saw the Baal Shem Tov pour a pile of gold coins on the table.

Immediately, the innkeeper called to his wife, and they began planning a wedding party for the young couple. The Baal Shem Tov reminded the innkeeper, "Don't forget, we want the best wine from your wine cellar for the celebration."

---

[57] Groom.
[58] Bride.

The next afternoon, there was a gala wedding at the inn. Word of the chasana passed through the nearby town, and the townsfolk flocked to the celebration. The Baal Shem Tov was the officiating Rabbi and his disciples took care of the other details of the marriage ceremony.

After the couple had been married under the Chupah,[59] the guests danced and ate and drank their fill. Then the Baal Shem Tov, sitting at a table with his followers said, "It is only right that the chosson and kallah receive gifts to begin their life together." The guests cheered and clapped their approval.

When they quieted down, the Baal Shem Tov continued, "And for my gift, I would like to give the chosson and the kallah this beautiful inn."

After a momentary silence, the innkeeper and his wife laughed so hard they could barely stand.

Then one of the followers, Reb Dov Ber (later known as the Mezritcher Maggid) chimed in, "And I would like to give them the flour mill down by the river."

"I will give the stables and horses by the inn," piped up Reb Ze'ev Kotses, another Chassid.

---

[59] Wedding canopy.

"And I will give the wine cellar in the inn," added another disciple.

Everyone at the wedding party turned to look at the innkeeper and his wife, and the Baal Shem Tov said, "And what about you innkeeper? What gift will you give to the newly married couple?"

"Oh, I will give them five rubles," said the innkeeper.

"Please," said the Baal Shem Tov, "that is not enough for a couple that has just had a big wedding at your inn."

"You are right," said the innkeeper, "I will give them the five thousand rubles of rent money that the Duke just collected from his land holdings."

The innkeeper's wife followed his words with, "And they can live in the old broken-down house at the end of town."

When the wedding guests murmured complaints about her stinginess, she said, "Okay, I will give the kallah the big diamond broach the Duke's wife always wears."

Then the wedding party benched and recited the Sheva Brochos[60] that are said after a wedding

---

[60] Seven blessings traditionally said after a wedding meal.

meal. The Baal Shem Tov quickly wrapped all the leftover food and drink into the table cloths that he had purchased from the innkeeper. The disciples put the leftovers into the little sled along with the newly-wedded chosson and kallah.

The Baal Shem Tov and the disciples got into their sled. Just before they departed, the Baal Shem Tov said to the young couple, "I give you a blessing that all of the blessings we bestowed on you will be fulfilled, and that you live long, healthy, happy lives both physically and spiritually and that you have children that follow in the ways of our holy Torah."

The newlyweds, still wearing their wedding clothes, got into their sled and started off along the road. At first, they were elated with the turn of events. They had been thrown out of the inn and, then, they had been married at the very same inn! They felt as though they had just awakened from a wonderful dream.

But after traveling a few hours, it dawned on them that they still had no place to go. And they still had no money. The joy from the wedding began to leave them and they began to feel worse and worse with the growing realization that they were in the same situation as before they had met Baal Shem Tov — except, of course, that now they were married and had food in the sled. As the hours passed and the tired old horse pulled their sled along a frozen Ukrainian road, they became more and more despondent.

Suddenly, the couple noticed an odd shape in the snow by the side of the road. It almost looked like a person! They got off the sled for a better look. "My G•d, it's a young nobleman," said Rivka. His skin was blue and icicles were forming on his beard. "Quick Shlomo," she instructed, "build a fire!"

Shlomo and Rivka covered the young nobleman with blankets put him next the by now blazing fire. When he regained consciousness, they gave him a drink of whiskey and fed him from the leftover food of the wedding.

As he slowly came back to himself, the young nobleman related how he had had an accident while hunting. He had fallen from his horse and his horse had run away.

Before he finished relating the story, the three of them heard the trumpeting of a hunting horn. Shortly thereafter, a servant of the young nobleman's father, the Duke, came riding up in search of the young man. As soon as he set eyes on him, the servant signaled for a carriage. The Duke's son got into the carriage, and they left without thanking or even acknowledging the newlyweds.

The Duke and the Duchess were hosting an extremely somber party to celebrate the collection of the Duke's rents. They and their entourage had returned from hunting that afternoon, only to learn that their son — their only child — was missing.

When the carriage carrying the young nobleman arrived at the castle, he was brought to his parents immediately. As he entered the party room, everyone cheered and breathed a sigh of relief. The boy was still in shock, and was taken to his room to recover. After some time, he came to himself and recalled how he had fallen from his horse and been saved by a young couple.

The young nobleman ran down to his parents to inquire about the couple that had saved his life. Everyone had forgotten about them.

"Quick! Find the couple and bring them here," the Duke instructed his servants. The servants rushed off, and found the couple. Their fire having died down and their food almost gone, Shlomo and Rivka had been sitting in their sled under blankets, once more unsure of their fate. They were brought to the castle and given a heroes' welcome.

The Duke questioned the couple, and learned of their being thrown out of the inn (which coincidently belonged to the Duke), their meeting with a strange Rabbi called the Baal Shem Tov, their wedding, and their finding the Duke and Duchess's son.

The Duke, the Duchess, their servants, and their guests were thrilled that the young man had been miraculously saved and had come to no harm. The music played and the liquor flowed, as they all crowded around the young couple, thanking them again and again.

Someone cried, "Let us help the newlyweds begin their life together with some gifts!" The Duke jumped up and said, "I am giving the newlyweds my inn, which is being run by that miserable innkeeper and his wife!"

When one of the royal party suggested that they be given the stables, the horses, and the wine cellar at the inn, the Duke responded, "Absolutely! All of that will be included."

Then another guest proposed, "What about the mill by the river?"

"Of course I agree. They are beautiful young people, and it is a wonderful idea," agreed the Duke.

"But won't they need cash?" offered the Duke's brother.

"Why, here is five thousand rubles — the rent I just collected from my tenants." And the Duke thrust a bag of gold coins into Shlomo's hand.

Then the Duchess removed her famous diamond broach and pinned it onto Rivka's wedding gown. She effused, "You are the most beautiful of all brides, and this is the least I can offer to thank you for giving me back my only son."

Then she hugged Rivka and began to weep.

"But what about the innkeeper and his wife?" Rivka asked. "Where will they live?"

"Oh, we will give them the broken-down house at the end of the town," answered the Duke's wife.

And so it was.

CHAPTER EIGHTEEN

CIRCUMCISION

NAMING AT A CIRCUMCISION

WHEN the Baal Shem Tov, then known as Yisrael, was still young and just married, he earned a meager livelihood by digging lime and taking it with his horse and wagon from town to town to sell. Although his holy wife, Rebbetzyn Channah, was bought up in a comfortable household and was not use to hard labor, she nevertheless helped Yisrael load the wagon and sometimes traveled with him for weeks on end. In the pale of Eastern Europe, they appeared as just another one of the numerous simple Jews.

After some time, their horse grew so weak that it was barely able to pull the wagon by itself much less when it was jam-packed with a heavy load. Yisrael grew worried: He could not afford a new horse and without one, he could not earn a living.

Once, he discussed his problem with some other poor travelers whom he met on the road. They told him there was a well-known Jewish landowner named Reb Boruch who lived in the community of Uman and was known for his hospitality. He also dealt in horses, so perhaps he could be of assistance to the young couple.

Yisrael and Channah traveled the long and tiring journey to see Reb Boruch.

Reb Boruch had fled the pogroms in his native Bohemia to Ukraine. Although not a Torah scholar, he studied Torah and lived as an observant Jew. Both he and his wife Rachel were kind, G•d-fearing people. They had two daughters and without other children decided to devote themselves and their wealth to charitable acts. They were particularly known for their involvement in the mitzvah of hospitality. They had built a special guesthouse on their estate that had many small rooms, each furnished with two beds and a table. Any needy traveler was welcome to stay for a week. The visitors were given two meals daily and on Shabbos joined all the other guests at Reb Boruch's table.

When a poor man came together with his wife and children, the family was given a room together. However, if a man and a woman came without children, Reb Boruch would not give them a room together because he was unsure not sure they were married. Finally, when the poor guests left, they were sent off with a charitable contribution to help them on their way.

When Yisrael and his wife Channah finally arrived at Reb Boruch's estate, they were offered a meal and a place to stay. After eating, Yisrael told his host about his horse. Reb Boruch immediately instructed his servants to replace it with a young, healthy horse. The gift was greatly appreciated and since the Yisrael and Channah were exhausted after their long journey, they decided to stay a few days until after Shabbos. Reb Boruch assigned them separate rooms according to his custom. "I don't doubt you are married, but my policy is not to give my guests a joint room unless I know for sure that they are a married couple," he explained. The Baal Shem Tov smiled at his explanation.

On Motzei Shabbos, as Reb Boruch sat pouring over a book of Torah, he looked up and noticed a bright light shining through a window from the guesthouse. He was afraid that maybe the guesthouse would catch fire and ran out to investigate. He quickly realized the light was not a fire, but a bright light coming from the window of one of the guest rooms.

He quietly approached the door of the room and peeked in through the keyhole. There he saw his unknown guest, sitting on the floor and reciting "Tikun Chatzos" — the midnight prayer lamenting the Destruction of the Holy Temple and the exile of the Divine Presence. The Baal Shem Tov's face was radiant and tears were pouring from his eyes. Next to him stood a tall man in a long robe with a long white beard and a glowing countenance. Reb Boruch fell down against the door in a faint. Hearing the commotion, the Baal Shem Tov rushed to the door and helped him into the room. After Reb Boruch composed himself, he fell down at the Baal Shem Tov's feet. "Please forgive me Rabbi for separating you from your wife."

The Baal Shem Tov helped Reb Boruch to his feet and answered, "Don't give it another thought. I can't thank you enough for your generosity. But I have one request: I ask that you promise me that you will not reveal anything you have seen tonight to anyone."

"Rebbe, I swear I will never tell anyone what I saw tonight," said Reb Boruch.

The Baal Shem Tov then said, "I bless you with a son that will grow up to be a great Tzaddik. Be sure that your wife nurses this child herself instead of using a wet nurse as she had done with your other children."

After responding, "Amen, may it be His will," to the Baal Shem Tov's blessing, Reb Boruch asked, "Rebbe, if I may be so bold as to ask, who was that old man all in white standing next to you?"

"Since you merited to see him," answered the Baal Shem Tov, "I'll reveal to you that it was the saintly Maharal (Rabbi Yehudah Leib ben Bezalel of

Prague). His lofty soul needs to return again to this world to accomplish some great tikkun. It is your privilege that this soul will find its abode in the son you will have. To this son you will give the name Leib. After his birth, I will see him and bless him."

Reb Boruch wept for joy because he had all but given up hope that he would ever have a son. "My holy master, please don't be angry with me, but may I ask what is your name and where are you from? I wish to help and provide for all your needs so you will never know need again."

"Please do not ask me these questions," responded the Baal Shem Tov, "for the time for me to be known in this world has not yet come. Your son likewise will not be known early in life. He will first live a life of poverty. Later, his righteousness will shine forth like the radiance of the sun. More than this I cannot tell you. And again I ask that you not tell anyone what you have seen and the words we have spoken here tonight. Please do not show me any special honor in anyone's presence, and treat me exactly as you do all the other guests you generously provide for. Tomorrow I will be on my way."

The Baal Shem Tov departed in his wagon, which was now harnessed to the new horse. No one knew what had transpired, but Reb Boruch recorded every detail in a diary.

Within a year, the Baal Shem Tov's blessing was fulfilled and Reb Boruch's wife gave birth to their first son. Their joy was boundless. Reb Boruch sent word to all the neighboring towns inviting all the poor to attend the bris and celebration. Because, as the Talmud says, "Your friend too has a friend," the message spread in no time, and groups of beggars started to travel to Uman to celebrate with Reb Boruch.

On the day of the bris, hundreds attended the joyful event. But Reb Boruch was anxious. He paced to and fro among the crowd looking for the face of the hidden Tzaddik whose blessing was the source of his son. Finally, he saw him coming with his staff and knapsack in the middle of a group of poor people. Reb Boruch ran to greet him, but did not manage to utter a word before the Baal Shem Tov motioned him to remain silent, adding: "Please be sure not to speak to me, nor to honor me in any special way. Simply treat me like all the other poor people here."

The bris was held after morning prayers, and the infant was named Aryeh Leib. Reb Boruch very much wanted the Baal Shem Tov to bless his new son, but realized he could not reveal his identity.

The custom in that city was when the male Kvater[61] was returning the child to the female Kvater, who in turn returned the baby to the baby's mother, they passed through the onlookers who gave blessings to the baby.

Just then, Reb Boruch thought of an idea. He had the Kvater carry his baby son throughout the crowd of people asking each person to give a blessing to the infant. Reb Boruch urged the Kvater to even carry the baby all the way through the crowd of poor folk because as he wished to have their blessings as well. As they approached the Baal Shem Tov, the latter placed his hands on the baby's head, and said in a loud and happy voice: "I am sorry — I am an ignorant man and don't know how to give blessings in the Holy Tongue. But I do remember one verse from the Torah that my father taught me:

"It says: V'Avhram Zaken — "And Avraham was old." The word 'av' at the beginning means father. The second word 'zaken' means 'zeide' (Yiddish for 'grandfather'). That is to say, our father Avraham is our grandfather. May this child be

---

[61] The female Kvater receives the baby from the baby's mother and gives him to her husband, the male Kvater, who then brings him to his father by the mohel.

blessed to grow up to be a grandfather for the entire Congregation of Yisrael, just as Avraham Avinu."

Some in the crowd were amused by the words of this simpleton. Some even laughed. Thereafter the joke remained — and the child was referred to as "Zeidelle" — the little grandfather. Townsfolk would jokingly ask Reb Boruch "How's your Zeidelle?" Even Reb Boruch and his wife called their son Zeidelle.

Indeed, the name remained throughout his life and Reb Aryeh Leib grew to become a great Tzaddik who helped his Jewish brethren and through acts of kindness in this World and through intercession in the World Above. Not only was he loved in his time, he is remembered to this day as the Shpoler Zeide — may his memory be a blessing.

And so it was.

MOSHIACH DAYS

THE EPISTLE[62]

TO my beloved brother-in-law, and my friend who is as dear to me as my own soul and heart, who is the distinguished rabbinic scholar, the Chassid, famous in the study of Torah and in his piety, his honor, our teacher, Rabbi Avraham Gershon, may his lamp shine, and peace be to all that is his. And to his modest wife Bluma and all her children, may they all be granted the blessing of life, Amen selah!

---

[62] The Epistle is a free translation of the letter that Rabbi Yisrael Baal Shem Tov wrote to his brother-in-law, Rabbi Gershon of Kitov, who was then living in the Holy Land. In the letter, the Baal Shem Tov describes his encounter with the Moshiach and what the latter said regarding the Baal Shem Tov's central role in causing the Moshiach to emerge in this world as the King of the Jewish Nation in the land of Yisrael. The Baal Shem Tov gave the letter to one of his closest followers, Rabbi Yaakov Yosef of Polonoye, to deliver to his brother-in-law, Rabbi Gershon. But because of circumstances, Rabbi Yaakov Yosef did not travel to the Land of Israel, and the letter remained in his hands so as to benefit the Children of Israel. This is one of the only writings believed to have actually been written by the Baal Shem Tov. The above is the Koretz version and it has been adapted to make it more readable.

I received your holy letter which you sent by the emissary from Jerusalem, at the fair in Loka in 5510 [1750]. It was written with extreme brevity. In it you said that you had already written at great length and sent the letters with someone who traveled by way of Egypt. However, those letters which were written at length did not reach me, and it caused me great anguish not to see what you wrote in detail with your holy handwriting.

Certainly this is because of the worsening conditions here and in nearby countries. Because of our many sins, the plague has spread to every country. It has even come close to here, in the holy community of Mohilov, and the districts of Walachia and Kedar.

Also, in your letter you said that those new interpretations and secrets which I wrote to you, through the scribe, the Rabbi and preacher of the holy community of Polonnoye, did not reach you. This too caused me great pain because you would have certainly derived great satisfaction from them. However, I have now forgotten certain parts of what I wrote. So I'm writing to you here, in brief, some details of what I remember.

On Rosh HaShanah of the Hebrew year 5507 (1747), I made an Aliyat HaNeshama (Ascent of the Soul) using the oath that you know. I saw amazing things in a vision, which I had not seen since I acquired my level of understanding. It would be impossible to tell you, even face to face, what I saw and learned during that ascent.

When I returned to the lower Gan Eden,[63] I saw the souls of the living and dead, some known to me and others unknown to me. They were without limit and number and they were running and returning by rising from world to world through the "Column" which is known to those initiated into the Kabbalah. They expressed such great and extensive joy, that the mouth is not able to express it and the physical ear is unable to hear it. Also, there were present many wicked people who had repented, and their sins were forgiven.

It was a time of great acceptance, and even to me, it was exceedingly amazing that so many were accepted by G•d in their repentance — some of them you too know. There was amongst them, also, very great joy, and they too rose up in the above-mentioned ascents. And they all begged me and pleaded with me to ascend together with them and be their helper and provider. They said "Your exalted Torah Eminence, the L•rd has granted you a special understanding to perceive and know these

---

63 Spiritual Garden of Eden.

matters." Because of the great joy which I saw amongst them, I decided to ascend with them.

And I saw in a vision that Satan had risen to accuse with great delight as never before. He issued decrees of forced conversion against a number of souls who would then be killed by unnatural deaths.

I was horrified and I actually risked my life to save them. I asked my Master and teacher[64] to go with me, for it is exceedingly dangerous to ascend to the upper worlds and since I arrived at my present level, I had not risen in such ascents.

I went up, level after level, until I entered the palace of the Moshiach, where the Moshiach studies Torah with all the Tannaim and the Righteous Ones, and with the Seven Shepherds. [65]I beheld very great joy there, but I did not know the reason for this extreme happiness.

I thought this joy was, G•d forbid, because of my demise from this world. But they told me later that I was not deceased and that they derived

---

[64] Achiyah HaShiloni.
[65] Avraham, Isaac, Jacob, Moses, Joshua, Aaron, and King David

tremendous pleasure when I performed Yichudim[66] in the world by means of the holy Torah. But as to the meaning of this great rejoicing, I still do not know.

And I asked the Moshiach, "When are you coming, my Master?"

He answered me, **"By this you shall know it: Once your teachings become publicly known and revealed throughout the world; and when your wellsprings have overflowed beyond, imparting to others what I have taught you and you have grasped; so that they too will be able to perform Yichudim and Ascents of the Soul as you do. Then all the kelipot will perish; and it will be a time of favor and salvation."**

I was bewildered at this response. I felt great anguish because of the length of time the Moshiach implied it would take until he came.

However while I was there, I learned three Segulos[67] and three Holy Names which were easy to learn and to explain to others. So I felt reassured, and I thought that perhaps, using these Segulos

---

[66] A form of kabalistic meditation based on different permutations and combinations of the Divine Names and attributes of G•d.

[67] Charm or remedy of spiritual potency.

and Holy Names, my Chevrayah Kaddisha might also be able to attain my spiritual level. That is, they would be able to practice Ascents of the Soul, and learn and understand the Supernal Mysteries as I do.

But I was not granted permission to reveal them during my life, and further, I asked on your behalf to teach them to you. But I was not permitted and I am under oath not to do this.

But this I can tell you. May the Blessed L•rd help you and may your paths be in G•d's presence and do not depart from them, especially in the Holy Land. While you are praying or studying, with every utterance and all that comes from your lips, intend to unify it with a Name of G•d because in every single letter there are Worlds and Souls and Divinity. And these letters rise and bind and unite with each other and in a true unity with G•dliness to form a word. And include your Soul with them in every level of the above. Then all the worlds will unite as one and rise up and make unaccountable joy and pleasure without limit.

If you can imagine the joy of the bride and groom, in its smallness and materiality, you can imagine how much more is the joy in the Upper World. Certainly the L•rd will "be thy help," and wherever you turn, you will prosper and succeed.

As it says, "Give to a wise man, and he will be yet wiser!" (*Proverbs 9:9*). Also, pray for me with the intention in your mind that I be privileged to share in the inheritance of the L•rd (*1 Samuel 26:19*) while I'm still alive; and also pray for the remnant of Israel that is outside the Land of Israel.

And I also asked there: "Why has the L•rd done this?; What does the heat of this great anger mean that so many Jewish souls were given over to Satan to be killed — and of them, a number who were baptized and then killed?" They gave me permission to ask Satan himself.

And so I asked Satan: "What is the point of this and what do you think of them converting and then being killed?"

He answered me, "My intention is for the sake of Heaven. And so it happened afterward, because of our many sins, that in the holy community of Zaslav there was a blood libel[68] against several souls. Two of them converted and were later killed, and the rest sanctified the Name of Heaven with great sanctity and died unnatural deaths. Then there were blood libels in the holy communities of Sibatuvka and Dunawitz, and there no one convert-

---

[68]Claiming that the Jews put Christian blood in the matzahs (unleavened bread) eaten during Passover.

193

ed after they had seen what happened in Zaslav. Rather, all of them gave over their lives for the sanctification of G•d. They sanctified the Name of Heaven and withstood the test. In the merit of this martyrdom, may our Moshiach come and take his vengeance and redeem his land and his people.

And on Rosh Hashanah of 5510 [1749], I performed an Ascent of the Soul using the oath you know, and I saw a great accusation against Yisrael, in which Satan was almost given permission to destroy entire countries and communities. I risked my life and prayed, "Let us fall by the Hand of the L•rd, and not by the hand of man." And they granted me permission to have the anti-Semitic persecutions exchanged for a great pestilence against animals and a plague against people the likes of which had not previously occurred in all the lands of Poland and other nearby countries. And that is exactly what happened. The pestilence spread to such an extent that it cannot be related. And the plague too spread in other countries.

After a long and engaged discussion as to what to do with my Chevrayah Kaddisha, we decided to recite the Ketores[69] in the morning prayers in

---

[69] Torah liturgy in the Siddur about incense (Ketores) used in the Bais HaMikdash (Holy Temple).

order to nullify the judgments mentioned above. Then it was revealed to me in a night vision, "But did not you yourself choose the plague, by saying, 'Let us fall by the hand of the L•rd,'" as mentioned above. "Why then do you wish to nullify the decree of the plague now? Surely an accuser cannot become a defender!

From then on I did not recite Ketores, and I did not pray about this. But on Hoshanah Rabbah, I went to the synagogue with the entire community, and I tried to intercede on behalf of Yisrael by means of several oaths because of my great fear for the safety of the Jewish community. I recited Ketores once so that the plague would not spread to our vicinity and was successful with the help of the L•rd.

I wanted to elaborate more and describe what happened at length, but because of my tears when I recall your departure from me, I am not able to speak. But I do ask you to review all my words of admonition which I told you several times. Let them always be in your thoughts, to meditate on them and ponder them thoroughly. Surely you will find in every word all kinds of sweetness, for what I told you is no vain thing. For the L•rd knows that I have not given up on journeying to the Land of Israel, if that be the Will of the L•rd, to be together with you.

But as of now, the time is not right for it.

Also, do not be too upset with me that I have not sent you money, for it is because of the desperate times we have had here with the plague and the famine. The young children of my family, as well as other poor Jews, are dependent upon me to support them and feed them. Our money is all spent . . . there is nothing left but our bodies! But the L•rd willing, when the L•rd shall enlarge . . . then certainly I'll send you money.

Also, my grandson, the young chosson, the honorable Ephraim, is a great Torah prodigy.

Surely if the time is right for it, how fitting it would be for you to come here so that we may see each other face to face and to rejoice in our happiness, as you promised me.

I also ask of you on behalf of the renowned Rabbi, the Chassid, our master Yosef Katz, a servant of the L•rd. Please befriend him and offer him all kinds of assistance for "all his deeds are for the sake of Heaven" and are welcome before the blessed L•rd. I also request of you to write on his behalf to the wealthy people to provide adequate support for him, for certainly he will be a source of satisfaction to you if he will be there with you.

Such are the words of your brother-in-law who looks forward to seeing you face to face and prays for a long life for you and your wife and your children, and seeks after your welfare daily and at night as well as for a good long life. Amen, Selah.

Yisrael Baal Shem Tov of the holy community of Mezibush

APPENDIX

GLOSSARY

Adam HaRishon — The first man.

Aggadata — sections of the Talmud interspersed with stories of the sages or elaboration of scriptural events.

Aliyah HaNeshama — Ascent of the Soul.

Ari HaKodesh — Arizal Rabbi Shlomo Itzhaki (1040-1105).

Avraham Avinu — The Patriarch Abraham our father.

Ayn Yaakov — A compilation of all the Aggadic material in the Talmud together with commentaries.

Baal Shem — Rabbi that utilized the powers of Kabbalah to heal the sick, ward off Demonic spirits and predict the future.

Baal Teshuvah — One who repents and returns to belief in G•d and the observance of the Mitzvos (Divine Commandments).

Baruch Hashem — Thank G•d.

Bat Mitzvah — Jewish girl reaches the age of maturity (12 years old) when she is responsible for her actions.

Beis Din — Jewish court.

Beis Hamikdosh — The Holy Temple.

Benching — Saying the Grace after meals.

Besht — Acronym for Baal Shem Tov.

Bimah — Readers stand.

Birchas Kohanim — Priestly blessing.

Bris — Circumcision.

Callah — The bride.

Challah — Braided bread eaten on Shabbos and festivals.

Chosson — The groom.

Chasana — A wedding.

GLOSSARY

Chassidus — Mystical explanations of the Torah.

Chazzan — Leader of communal prayer.

Cheder — Hebrew day school for young boys.

Chaburah — Group of friends.

Chevrayah Kaddisha — Group of Holy friends.

Chuppah — A wedding canopy.

Chumash — Five books of Moses.

Darshan — One who expounds on the Midrashic teachings of the Torah.

Daven — Pray.

Dveikus — Cleaving to G•d.

Eliyahu HaNavi — Elijah the Prophet.

Festivals — Rosh HaShanah, Yom Kippur, Succos, Pesach, etc.

Gabbai — Custodian of the shule.

Gartle — A prayer belt worn by Chassidim.

Gemorrah — Component of the Talmud comprising rabbinical analysis of and commentary on the Mishnah.

Get — Bill of divorce.

Goan Olam — World class Torah scholar.

Ha Kodesh Boruch Hu — The Holy One Blessed be He.

HaMotzi — Prayer said over bread.

HaShem — The Name (G•d).

Havdalah — A ritual prayer recited at the close of Shabbos and other holy days that marks the separation between holy days and the ordinary days of the week.

Ilui — Genius.

Ineffable Name — 72 letter name of G•d.

Kabbalah — The teachings and doctrines that deal with the Jewish Mystical Tradition.

Kallah — A bride.

Kameya — An amulet.

Kashrus — Food in accord with Jewish law, termed kosher in English.

Kavanah (kavanos) — Intention or direction of the heart.

GLOSSARY

Kelipot — "Husk" in Kabbalistic thought, is the aspect of evil or impurity that obscures the holy and good.

Kiddush — The ritual of sanctification of Shabbos or Yom Tov, usually recited over a cup of wine.

Klaf — Animal skin used for holy scrolls such as Mezuzahs and Tefillin.

Kvittel — A note in which the petitioner writes out his or her request.

Maariv — The evening prayer service.

Machpelah — A cave in Hebron where Adam and Eve, Abraham and Sarah, Isaac and Rebecca, and Yaakov and Leah are buried.

Mashka — Liquor.

Matronita — The Shechina — the female aspect of G•d.

Melavah Malkah — Meal eaten after the conclusion of the Shabbos that celebrates the return of the Shabbos Queen to heaven, where she dwells until the next Shabbos, when she returns once again.

Melamed — Hebrew teacher for young boys.

Mesirus nefesh — Great self sacrifice.

Mincha — The afternoon prayer service.

Minyan — Ten Jewish men needed for communal prayer.

Mishnah — Frequently used to designate the Jewish law which was transmitted orally.

Mitzvos — Divine commandments.

Mikveh — Pool for ritual immersion.

Mitzvah — Divine commandment.

Moshe Rabbeinu — Moses our teacher.

Moshiach — Messiah.

Neshamah — G•dly Soul.

Neshamah Chadasha — A new soul that had not previously occupied a physical body.

Niggun — Spiritual melody without words.

Parnassah — Money livelihood.

Posul — Not kosher.

Rasha — Wicked person.

Rashi — Rabbi Shlomo Itzhaki (1040 — 1105).

GLOSSARY

Reb — Title of respect like Mister, usually followed by the person's forename.

Rebbe — Spiritual master and leader of a Chassidic Sect.

Rosh Chodesh — First day of Jewish month.

Rosh yeshiva — Head of a yeshiva.

Satan — Angel that serves as the Adversary.

Shehecheyanu — The blessing of Shehecheyanu, meaning "Who has given us life", is recited in thanks when doing or experiencing something that occurs infrequently and from which one derives pleasure or benefit.

Sefer — Sacred Hebrew Book.

Segulah — Charm or remedy of mystical potency.

Seudah — Meal.

Seudah Shlishis — The third meal, traditionally eaten on Shabbos before sunset.

Shabbos — Jewish for the Sabbath.

Shadchan — Matchmaker.

Shalom Aleichem — Peace be to you.

Shalosh Seudos — The third meal, traditionally eaten on Shabbos before sunset.

Shamash — Synagogue caretaker.

Shechinah — The female aspect of G•d.

Shochet — A Jewish slaughterer that kills the animals in accordance with the requirements of Jewish law.

Shule — Synagogue.

Siddur — The book of daily ritual Hebrew prayers.

Simcha — Joyous celebration.

Shtetl — Small town.

Tallis — Prayer shawl.

Tannaim — Jewish Sages of the Mishnah 10 CE — 220 CE.

Tefillin — Also called phylacteries are two small cubic leather boxes painted black, containing scrolls of parchment inscribed with verses from the Torah, strapped to head and arm with black leather straps typically worn by Jewish men during week-day morning prayers.

Tehillim — Psalms.

Teshuvah — Repentance; literally turning back to G•d.

Tikune Zohar — A book of Kabbalah.

Tish — Literally a table in Jewish. Among Chassidim, a tish refers to any joyous public celebration or gathering or meal by Chassidim at a "table" of their Rebbe.

Torah — Twenty Four canonized scriptures of traditional Judaism. It consists of the Five Books of Moses, the Prophets, and the Writings. The Torah can also mean any spiritual text book or idea that is connected to traditional Judaism.

Treife — Non-kosher.

Tu Bshvat — A holiday occurring on the 15th of the Hebrew month of Shvat celebrating the New Year of the trees.

Tzaddik — Holy man.

Tzaddik nistar — a hidden holy man.

Tzedeka — Charity.

Upscherinish — The first cutting of a boys hair at three years old.

Yahrtzeit —The anniversary of the death of a loved one.

Yetzer Hara — Evil Inclination.

Yechudim — "Yichudim" are a form of kabalistic meditation based on different permutations and combinations of the Divine Names and attributes of G•d.

Yechidus — Private audience with a Rebbe.

Zaida — Grandfather in Yiddish.

BIBLIOGRAPHY

1. BAAL SHEM TOV GENESIS Vol. I by Tzvi Meir Cohn

2. BAAL SHEM TOV EXODUS Vol. II by Tzvi Meir Cohn

3. BAAL SHEM TOV LEVITICUS Vol. III by Tzvi Meir Cohn .

4. BAAL SHEM TOV NUMBERS Vol. IV by Tzvi Meir Cohn

5. BAAL SHEM TOV DEUTERONOMY Vol. V by Tzvi Meir Cohn

6. BAAL SHEM TOV FAITH LOVE AND JOY Vol. I by Tzvi Meir Cohn

7. BAAL SHEM TOV DIVINE LIGHT Vol. II by Tzvi Meir Cohn

8. BAAL SHEM TOV HEART OF PRAYER Vol. III by Tzvi Meir Cohn

9. IN PRAISE OF THE BAAL SHEM TOV Translated and edited by Ben Amos and Mintz

10. STORIES OF THE BAAL SHEM TOV
by Rabbi Yisrael Yaakov Klapholtz
11. A TREASURY OF CHASSIDIC TALES ON THE
FESTIVALS
by Rabbi Shlomo Yoseph Zevin
12. A TREASURY OF CHASSIDIC TALES ON THE
TORAH
by Rabbi Shlomo Yoseph Zevin
13. SEEKER OF SLUMBERING SOULS
by Rabbi Zalman Ruderman
14. THE PATH OF THE BAAL SHEM TOV
by Rabbi David Sears
15. ESSENTIAL PAPERS ON CHASSIDISM
Edited by Gershon David Hundert
16. MEETINGS WITH REMARKABLE SOULS
by Rabbi Eliyahu Klein
17. CLASSIC CHASSIDIC TALES
by Meyer Levin
18. STORY TELLING AND SPIRITUALITY IN
JUDAISM
by Maggid Yitzhak Buxbaum
19. THE LIGHT BEYOND
by Rabbi Aryeh Kaplan
20. TZAVA'AT HARIVASH
by Rabbi Jacob Immanuel Shochet

21. THE LIGHT AND FIRE OF THE BAAL SHEM
    TOV
    by Maggid Yitzhak Buxbaum
22. THE BAAL SHEM TOV
    by Professor Emanuel Etkes
23. EXTRAORDINARY CHASSIDIC TALES
    by Rabbi Rafael Nachman Kahn
24. THE GREAT MISSION
    by Rabbi Eli Friedman
25. CHASSIDIC MASTERS
    by Rabbi Aryeh Kaplan
26. THE RELIGIOUS THOUGHT OF CHASSIDIM
    by Rabbi Norman Lamm
27. CHASSIDIC TALES
    by Rabbi Rami Shapiro
28. RABBI ISRAEL BAAL SHEM TOV
    by Rabbi Jacob Immanuel Shochet
29. THE SLAVE WHO SAVED THE CITY
    by Harry M. Rabinowicz
30. THE STORY OF THE BAAL SHEM TOV
    by Dr. J. L. Snitzer
31. THE LEGEND OF THE BAAL SHEM
    By Martin Buber
32. ESSENTIAL PAPERS ON HASIDISM
    by Gershon David Hundert
33. FOUNDER OF HASIDISM
    by Moshe Rosman

34. MIRACLE MEN
   by David L. Meckler

SOURCES OF
THE BAAL SHEM TOV STORIES

Chapter One [SHABBOS]
THE SHABBOS GUEST

Freely adapted by Tzvi Meir HaCohane Cohn from stories found in:

SHIVCHEI HABAAL SHEM TOV and translated in IN PRAISE OF THE BAAL SHEM TOV by Ben Amos and Mintz.

SEEKERS OF SLUMBERING SOULS by Rabbi Moshe Rabin.

THE LIGHT AND FIRE OF THE BAAL SHEM TOV by Yitzhak Buxbaum.

SHABBOS JOY

Freely adapted by Tzvi Meir HaCohane Cohn from a story found in STORIES OF THE BAAL SHEM Tov by Rabbi Y.Y. Klapholtz.

Chapter Two [ROSH HASHANAH]
HOW TO BLOW A SHOFAR

Freely adapted by Tzvi Meir HaCohane Cohn from a story found in TREASURY OF CHASSIDIC TALES by Rabbi S.Y. Zevin.

L'CHAYIM

Freely adapted by Tzvi Meir HaCohane Cohn from a story adapted by Rabbi Yrachmiel Tilles of Ascent Institute from the rendition of Rabbi Tuvia Bolton of Yeshiva Ohr Tmimim.

Chapter Three [SHABBOS TESHUVAH]
SHABBOS TESHUVAH

Freely adapted by Tzvi Meir HaCohane Cohn from a story found in TREASURY OF CHASSIDIC TALES by Rabbi S.Y. Zevin.

Freely adapted by Tzvi Meir HaCohane Cohn from stories found in THE LIGHT AND FIRE OF THE BAAL SHEM TOV by Yitzhak Buxbaum from KOL SIPPUREI BAAL SHEM TOV, vol 2., from SIFREI BAAL SHEM TOV.

Chapter Four [YOM KIPPUR]
COCK-A-DOODLE-DO!

Freely adapted by Tzvi Meir HaCohane Cohn from a story found in TREASURY OF CHASSIDIC TALES ON THE FESTIVALS by Rabbi S.Y. Zevin.

A MODERN DAY BAAL SHEM TOV STORY

Freely adapted by Tzvi Meir HaCohane Cohn from a story reprinted by Ascent of Safed from KEEPING IN TOUCH by Rabbi Eliyahu Touger, published by Sichos In English.

Chapter Five [SUCCOS]
A DRY SUCCAH

Freely adapted by Tzvi Meir HaCohane Cohn from a story found in TREASURY OF CHASSIDIC TALES ON THE FESTIVALS by Rabbi S.Y. Zevin.

THE SUCCAH OF REB PINCHAS OF KORETZ

Freely adapted by Tzvi Meir Cohane Cohn from a story in SIPUREI BAAL SHEM TOV as translated in STORIES OF THE BAAL SHEM TOV by Y.Y. Klapholtz.

Chapter Six [SIMCHAS TORAH]
THE EXCHANGE

Freely adapted by Tzvi Meir Cohane Cohn from a story in SIPUREI BAAL SHEM TOV as translated in STORIES OF THE BAAL SHEM TOV by Y.Y. Klapholtz.

CANOPY OF FIRE

Freely adapted by Tzvi Meir HaCohane Cohn from a story in SHIVCHEI HABAAL SHEM TOV and translated in IN PRAISE OF THE BAAL SHEM TOV by Ben Amos and Mintz.

Chapter Seven [TU B'SHVAT]
THE MYSTICAL ORANGE GROVE

Freely adapted by Tzvi Meir HaCohane Cohn from a story translated in THE LIGHT AND FIRE OF THE BAAL SHEM TOV by Maggid Yitzchak Buxbaum.

Chapter Eight [CHANUKAH]
THE CHANUKAH LIGHTS

Freely adapted by Tzvi Meir HaCohane from a story in MA'ASEH B'RABBI YISRAEL BAAL SHEM TOV as translated in THE LIGHT AND FIRE OF THE BAAL SHEM TOV by Maggid Yitzchak Buxbaum.

Chapter Nine [PURIM]
A SWEET SONG

Freely adapted by Tzvi Meir HaCohane Cohn from a story written by HaRav, HaChosid, Dr. Nissan Mindel.

Chapter Ten [SHABBOS HAGADOL]
THE DANCING BEAR

Freely adapted by Tzvi Meir HaCohane Cohn from a story in SHIVCHEI HABAAL SHEM TOV and translated in IN PRAISE OF THE BAAL SHEM TOV by Ben Amos and Mintz.

Chapter Eleven [PASSOVER]
PASSOVER IN ISTANBUL

Freely adapted by Tzvi Meir HaCohane Cohn from a story found in ADAS TZADDIKIM and translated in STORIES OF THE BAAL SHEM TOV by Y.Y. Klapholtz.

THE WIFE IS RIGHT

Freely adapted by Tzvi Meir HaCohne Cohn from a story found in SEEKER OF SLUMBERING SOULS by Rabbi Moshe Rabin.

Chapter Twelve [SEVENTH DAY OF PASSOVER]
TRUE FAITH

Freely adapted by Tzvi Meir HaCohane Cohn from a letter from the Rav of Mezibush as translated in STORIES OF THE BAAL SHEM TOV by Y.Y. Klapholtz.

Chapter Thirteen [LAG B'OMER]
THE LAG B'OMER PARADE

Freely adapted by Tzvi Meir HaCohane Cohn from SICHAT HASHAVUA #176, as translated by Rabbi Yerachmiel Tilles of the Ascent Center in Safed, Yisrael.

Chapter Fourteen [SHAVUOS]
A MATTER OF STRENGTH

Freely adapted by Tzvi Meir HaCohane Cohn from a story found in A TREASURY OF CHASSIDIC TALES ON THE FESTIVALS by Rabbi S.Y. Zevin.

THE LAST REVELATION

Freely adapted by Tzvi Meir HaCohane Cohn from a story in SHIVCHEI HABAAL SHEM TOV and translated in IN PRAISE OF THE BAAL SHEM TOV by Ben Amos and Mintz.

Chapter Fifteen [CHAI ELUL]
THE SOUL OF THE BAAL SHEM TOV

Freely adapted by Tzvi Meir HaCohane Cohn from a story in HATAMIM as translated in STORIES OF THE BAAL SHEM TOV by Y. Y. Klapholtz.

THE BIRTH OF THE ALTER REBBE

Freely adapted by Tzvi Meir Cohane Cohn from a story in HATAMIM as translated in STORIES OF THE BAAL SHEM TOV by Y.Y. Klapholtz.

Chapter Sixteen [BIRTHDAY]
BIRTHDAY WITH ELIYAHU HANAVI

Freely adapted by Tzvi Meir Cohane Cohn from a story in SHIVCHEI HABAAL SHEM TOV as translated in IN PRAISE OF THE BAAL SHEM TOV by Ben Amos and Mintz.

Chapter Seventeen [MARRIAGE]
THE WEDDING BLESSINGS

Freely adapted by Tzvi Meir Cohane Cohn from a story in EXTRAORDINARY CHASSIDIC TALES by Rabbi R. N. Kahn.

Chapter Eighteen [CIRCUMCISION]
NAMING AT A CIRCUMCISION

Freely adapted by Tzvi Meir Cohane Cohn from a story in A TREASURY OF CHASSIDIC TALES ON THE TORAH by Rabbi S.Y. Zevin.

Chapter Nineteen [MOSHIACH DAYS]
THE EPISTLE

Freely adapted by Tzvi Meir Cohane Cohn from THE BESHT by Professor Emanuel Etkes; THE RELIGIOUS THOUGHT OF CHASSIDIM by Rabbi Norman Lamm; and THE PATH OF THE BAAL SHEM TOV by Rabbi David Sears.

The following is the original from IGROS KODESH
Vol. 6 written by the Previous Rebbe[70]

וכהמעשה חידוע:

חוד כ"ק אאזמו"ר הרה"ק צמח צדק זצוקללה"ה נבג"מ זי"ע הואיל
לשלוח את הרב הגאון האמיתי החסיד הנודע מוה"ר יצחק אייזיק נ"ע
הלוי עפשטיין מהאמליע לכ"ק אדמו"ר מוה"ר ישראל מרוזין
זצוקללה"ה נבג"מ זי"ע בהנוגע לעניו הכלל.

החסיד הר"א להיותו מחניכי חסידי חב"ד התענין במאד לדעת את
ארחות והנהגות חסידי רוזין בכלל והנהגותיו של כ"ק ר' ישראל מרוזין
בפרט וישם דעתו הרחבה ולבו על כל דבר הנהגה בפרט.

הסדר אצל כ"ק ר' ישראל מרוזין חי' אשר בעת קבלת שלום –
הנהוג אצל חסידי פולין ואהלין – וכן בשעת קבלת אנשים – פראוועֶן
זיך – וקריאת הפתקאות – קוויטלעך – הנה המקורב – אחד מיחידי
סגולה מזקני החסידים אשר בחר בו כ"ק ר' ישראל להיות המתורגמן
בינו ובין החסידים והי' מכונה בשם מקורב – חי' עומד על ימינו וגבאי
הראשון משמאלו.

בין האורחים שהיו אז ברוזין חי' אחד מגדולי הרבנים בבוקאווינא
מפורסם ללמדן גדול וממקושריו הכי גדולים של כ"ק ר' ישראל והביא
את חבורו לקבל עליו הסכמתו של כ"ק ר' ישראל, וגם אחד החסידים
בא אשר אסף כמה כמה שנים ספורי מעשיות מצדיקים וחסידים ויבוא גם
הוא את חבורו לקחת הסכמה מכ"ק ר' ישראל.

בשעת קבלת האנשים עמדו שני החסידים המקושרים הנ"ל, הרב
והחסיד, וחבוריהם בידיהם. המקורב – ע"פ הוראת כ"ק ר' ישראל –
לקח את ספריהם מידיהם ויקרא לפני כ"ק ר' ישראל איזה מקומות
מחבורו של הרב ואח"כ קרא איזה ספורים מספרו של החסיד המלקט.

כ"ק ר' ישראל ישב בדבקות ואח"כ התחיל לדבר בדבר מעלת
ספורי צדיקים וחרושם הגדול שדבר זה עושה בהיכלי הצדיקים בגן
עדן, ואח"כ דיבר בעניני חדושי תורה באותם הענינים אשר המקורב
קרא לפניו מספרו של הרב בפלפול רב, ואח"כ צוה להמקורב לכתוב
את הסכמתו על שני הספרים.

החסיד החב"די הרי"א נ"ע הסתכל בתשומת לב על הסדר בקבלת
האנשים ועל יחס כ"ק ר' ישראל למקושריו ויתפלא על עומק הפלפול
וסגנונו שחידש כ"ק ר' ישראל בחדושי התורה של הרב, אבל הי'
מוקשה לו מדוע הקדים כ"ק ר' ישראל את הערותיו וכן את הצווי
לכתוב את הסכמתו לספר הלקוטים של ספורי המעשיות להערותיו

---

[70]Rabbi Yosef Yitzchak Schneerson [1880-1950] the
sixth Rebbe of Chabad-Lubavitch.

~Dedications~

IN SINCERE APPRECIATION AND
GRATITUDE FOR
RABBI MENACHEM MENDEL SCHNEERSON
THE LUBAVITCH REBBE SHLITA
MAY HIS SPIRITUAL GUIDANCE CONTINUE TO
LEAD AND GUIDE AND DIRECT US ALONG THE
CORRECT PATH FOR SPIRITUAL AND PHYSICAL
SUCCESS IN OUR LIVES AND THOSE OF OUR
FAMILY UNTIL THE COMPLETE AND FINAL
REDEMPTION THROUGH OUR
RIGHTEOUS MOSHIACH

~Dedications~

IN BLESSED MEMORY OF THE

LUBAVITCH REBBE SHLITA

MAY HIS PRAYERS AND OUR GOOD DEEDS

SPEEDILY USHER IN FOR US THE COMPLETE

AND FINAL REDEMPTION THROGH OUR

RIGHTEOUS MOSHIACH

IN HONOR OF OUR WONDERFUL CHILDREN

LEAH, SARAH AND RACHEL

BY THEIR LOVING PARENTS

DAN AND AMY KARNS

~Dedications~

IN APPRECIATION TO HASHEM FOR THE MERIT
TO SHARE IN THIS MAGNIFICENT WORK WITH
OUR SONS ADAM AND JACOB
LOVE BRYAN AND RAIZEL MICHELOW

IN SINCERE GRATITUDE TO HASHEM
IN HONOR OF THE
THIRD WEDDING ANNIVERSARY OF
YOSSI AND ELISHEVA BIALO

IN LOVING MEMEORY OF OUR BELOVED FATHER
YITZCHAK LEIB BEN YISRAEL & FRUMA RIVKA
LOUIS JAFFE
HE LOVED LIFE AND LOVED PEOPLE
BY HIS CHILDREN

~Dedications~

IN MEMORY OF THE
CHASSID CHAIM ELIEZER BEN YAAKOV SHIMON

IN MEMORY OF
ZEV MEIR BEN YAAKOV SHIMON AND
ITA RAIZA BAS NOSSON
CHASSID CHAIM ELIEZER BEN YAAKOV SHIMON

TO HASHEM WHO IS THE SOURCE
OF EVERYTHING AND TO OUR CHILDREN
JOSHUA, MATTHEW AND JENNA
HOWARD AND SUSAN KOSSOFF

WITH LOVE AND AWE OF HASHEM
BLESSINGS FOR JON KAPLAN AND HIS
FAMILY

I

WWW.MEZUZAH.NET

Home of the World Wide
Mezuzah Campaign

The fundamental goal of The World Wide Mezuzah Campaign is to unify the Jewish people. By fulfilling the mitzvah of Mezuzah, this unity can be accomplished by each Jewish person: man, woman or child. The mitzvah can be easily fulfilled by affixing a Mezuzah on the "Doorpost of Your House or upon Your Gates," as required by Jewish law.

Purchase Mezuzahs written in Yisrael by a Certified Scribe, then checked by a computer for accuracy and finally checked by a second Certified Scribe before we send it to you. Our Mezuzahs are of a very high quality, and they are beautifully written. They are shipped to you in a Mezuzah case ready to mount on your door.

www.mezuzah.net
The World Wide Mezuzah Campaign.
A project of the Baal Shem Tov Foundation
a 501(c)(3), non-profit organization

Baal Shem Tov Times

Spreading the light of the legendary
Kabbalah Master and Mystic

Rabbi Yisrael Baal Shem Tov

-A weekly email publication-

Regular Features:

Baal Shem Tov Story
Torah Baal Shem Tov
Heart of Prayer
Divine Light
Kesser Shem Tov

Subscribe to receive your FREE weekly
e-mail edition at
www.baalshemtov.com

ABOUT THE AUTHOR

Tzvi Meir (Howard M.) Cohn is a Patent and Trademark Attorney (www.CohnPatents.com). He attended Yeshiva Hadar Hatorah in Crown Heights, Brooklyn after completing his university studies in Engineering and Law. While studying at the Yeshiva, he discovered a deep connection to the stories and teachings of the Baal Shem Tov. More recently, he founded the Baal Shem Tov Foundation which is dedicated to spreading the teachings of the Baal Shem Tov throughout the world in order to hasten the coming of the Moshiach. To spread the teachings of the Baal Shem Tov, Tzvi Meir created a website, www.BaalShemTov.com and publishes a weekly newsletter, The Baal Shem Tov Times. Also, Tzvi Meir initiated the World Wide Mezuzah Campaign (www.Mezuzah.net) as a project of the Baal Shem Tov Foundation. Tzvi Meir gives live presentations of his original music and Baal Shem Tov stories to welcoming audiences.

OTHER BOOKS BY

TZVI MEIR HACOHANE COHN

BAAL SHEM TOV FAITH LOVE AND JOY Vol. I

BAAL SHEM TOV DIVINE LIGHT Vol. II

BAAL SHEM TOV HEART OF PRAYER Vol. III

BAAL SHEM TOV GENESIS Vol. I

BAAL SHEM TOV EXODUS Vol. II

BAAL SHEM TOV LEVITICUS Vol. III

BAAL SHEM TOV NUMBERS Vol. IV

BAAL SHEM TOV DEUTERONOMY Vol. V

081212

www.ingramcontent.com/pod-product-compliance
Lightning Source LLC
LaVergne TN
LVHW011221080426
835509LV00005B/242